CONTENTS

Hugo's Simplified System

German
Phrase Book

Hugo's Language Books Ltd, London

This edition
© 1986 Hugo's Language Books Ltd/Lexus Ltd
All rights reserved
ISBN 0 85285 083 2

Compiled by
Lexus Ltd
with
Chris Stephenson
and
Horst Kopleck

*Facts and figures given in this book were
correct when printed. If you discover any
changes, please write to us.*

Reprinted 1987

Set in 9/9 Plantin Light by
Typesetters Ltd and
printed in England by
Anchor Brendon Ltd

PREFACE

This is the latest in a long line of Hugo Phrase Books and is of excellent pedigree, having been compiled by experts to meet the general needs of tourists and business travellers. Arranged under the usual headings of 'Hotels', 'Motoring' and so forth, the ample selection of useful words and phrases is supported by an 1800-line mini-dictionary. By cross-reference to this, scores of additional phrases may be formed. There is also an extensive menu guide listing approximately 600 dishes or methods of cooking and presentation.

The pronunciation of words and phrases in the main text is imitated in English sound syllables, and highlighted sections illustrate some of the replies you may be given and the signs or instructions you may see or hear.

PRONUNCIATION

When reading the imitated pronunciation, stress that part which is underlined. Pronounce each syllable as if it formed part of an English word, and you will be understood sufficiently well. Remember the points below, and your pronunciation will be even closer to the correct German. Use our audio cassette of selected extracts from this book, and you should be word-perfect!

KH represents the guttural German 'ch' and should sound like the Scottish 'loch' (which isn't 'lock').

OO represents the longer German 'u'; make this an English 'oo' as in 'food' (not short as in 'foot').

oo represents the shorter German 'u', as in English 'took', 'book'.

œ is how we imitate the German 'ü', which sounds like the 'ee' in 'seen' if you pronounce it with rounded lips (or like the French 'u').

ow should sound like the 'ow' in 'cow' (not as in 'low').

USEFUL EVERYDAY PHRASES

Yes/No
Ja/Nein
ya/nine

Thank you
Danke
dank-uh

No thank you
Nein danke
nine dank-uh

Please
Bitte
bitt-uh

I don't understand
Ich verstehe nicht
iKH fare-shtay-uh niKHt

Do you speak English/French/Spanish/Italian?
Sprechen Sie Englisch/Französisch/Spanisch/Italienisch?
shpreKHen zee eng-lish/frantser-zish/shpah-nish/italyane-ish

I can't speak German
Ich spreche kein Deutsch
iKH shpreKH-uh kine doytsh

Please speak more slowly
Bitte sprechen Sie etwas langsamer
bitt-uh shpreKHen zee etvas langzammer

USEFUL EVERYDAY PHRASES

Good morning/good afternoon/good night
Guten Morgen/Guten Tag/Gute Nacht
gOOten morgen/gOOten tahk/gOOt-uh naKHt

Goodbye
Auf Wiedersehen
owf-veeder-zane

How are you?
Wie geht es Ihnen?
vee gate ess een-en

Excuse me please
Entschuldigung
entshooldigoong

Sorry!
Verzeihung!
fare-tseye-oong

I'm really sorry
Es tut mir wirklich leid
ess toot mere veerkliKH lite

Can you help me?
Können Sie mir helfen?
kernen zee mere helfen

Can you tell me...?
Können Sie mir sagen...?
kernen zee mere zah-gen

Where is the lavatory please?
Wo ist die Toilette bitte?
vo ist dee twalet-uh bitt-uh

Can I have...?
Kann ich ... haben?
kan iKH ... ha-ben

I would like...
Ich möchte gern...
iKH merKHt-uh gairn

Is there ... here?
Gibt es hier...?
gipt ess here

Where can I get...?
Wo kann ich ... bekommen?
vo kan iKH ... bukommen

How much is it?
Was kostet das?
vas kostet das

Can I pay by cheque?
Kann ich per Scheck bezahlen?
kan iKH pair sheck butsahlen

Do you take credit cards?
Akzeptieren Sie Kreditkarten?
aktsepteeren zee kredeet-karten

What time is it?
Wie spät ist es?
vee spayte ist ess

I must go now
Ich muß jetzt gehen
iKH mooss yetst gay-en

Cheers!
Prost!
prohst

Go away!
Verschwinden Sie!
fairshvinden zee

THINGS YOU'LL SEE OR HEAR

Abfahrt	departure
Achtung	attention
Ankunft	arrival
auf	open
Ausgang	way out
außer Betrieb	out of order
besetzt	engaged
bezahlen	to pay
bis	until
bitte	please
bitte nicht...	do not...
Damen	ladies
drehen	to turn
drücken	to push
Durchgang	passage
Eingang	way in
eintreten	to enter
Eintritt	entry
Erwachsene	adults
frei	free
Fußgänger	pedestrians
Gebühren	charges
Gefahr	danger
geöffnet	open
geschlossen	closed
halt	stop
Herren	gentlemen
hinten	at the back
Kasse	till, cash desk
kein	no, not any
Kinder	children
klingeln	to ring
klopfen	to knock
Kontrolle	check, inspection

11

langsam	slow
links	left
nicht...	don't...
Nichtraucher	no smoking
oben	at the top
offen	open
Öffnungszeiten	opening hours
Paß	passport
Preis	price
Raucher	smokers
rechts	right
reserviert	reserved
schnell	fast
Stadt	town, city
strafbar	punishable
Straße	road, street
Stufe	step
Toilette	toilet
über	over, above
unten	at the bottom
unter	under
verboten	prohibited
verkaufen	to sell
vermieten	to rent
von	from, of
vorn	at the front
Vorsicht	take care
Zeit	time
ziehen	to pull
Zoll	Customs
zu	shut, to
Zugang	access
Zutritt	entry

DAYS, MONTHS, SEASONS

Sunday	Sonntag	*zontahk*
Monday	Montag	*mohn-tahk*
Tuesday	Dienstag	*deens-tahk*
Wednesday	Mittwoch	*mit-voKH*
Thursday	Donnerstag	*donners-tahk*
Friday	Freitag	*fry-tahk*
Saturday	Samstag	*zams-tahk*
	Sonnabend	*zon-ahbent*
January	Januar	*yanOOah*
February	Februar	*faybrOOah*
March	März	*mairts*
April	April	*aprill*
May	Mai	*my*
June	Juni	*yOOnee*
July	Juli	*yOOlee*
August	August	*ow-goost*
September	September	*zeptember*
October	Oktober	*oktober*
November	November	*november*
December	Dezember	*daytsember*
Spring	Frühling	*frœling*
Summer	Sommer	*zommer*
Autumn	Herbst	*hairpst*
Winter	Winter	*vinter*
Christmas	Weihnachten	*vye-naKHten*
Christmas Eve	Heiligabend	*highliKH-ahbent*
Good Friday	Karfreitag	*karfry-tahk*
Easter	Ostern	*ohstern*
New Year	Neujahr	*noy-yah*
New Year's Eve	Silvester	*zilvester*
Whitsun	Pfingsten	*pfingsten*

NUMBERS

0 null *nool*
1 eins *eynss*
2 zwei *tsvy*
3 drei *dry*
4 vier *feer*
5 fünf *fœnf*
6 sechs *zex*
7 sieben *zeeben*
8 acht *aKHt*
9 neun *noyn*
10 zehn *tsane*
11 elf *elf*
12 zwölf *tsverlf*
13 dreizehn *drytsane*
14 vierzehn *feertsane*
15 fünfzehn *fœnftsane*
16 sechzehn *zeKHtsane*
17 siebzehn *zeeptsane*
18 achtzehn *aKHtsane*
19 neunzehn *noyntsane*
20 zwanzig *tsvantsiKH*
21 einundzwanzig *ine-oont-tsvantsiKH*
22 zweiundzwanzig *tsvy-oont-tsvansiKH*
30 dreißig *drysiKH*
40 vierzig *feertsiKH*
50 fünfzig *fœnftsiKH*
60 sechzig *zeKHtsiKH*
70 siebzig *zeeptsiKH*
80 achtzig *aKHttsiKH*
90 neunzig *noyntsiKH*
100 hundert *hoondert*
110 hundertzehn *hoondert-tsane*
200 zweihundert *tsvy-hoondert*
1000 tausend *towzent*
1,000,000 eine Million *ine-uh mill-yohn*

TIME

today	heute	*hoyt-uh*
yesterday	gestern	*gestern*
tomorrow	morgen	*morgen*
the day before yesterday	vorgestern	*forgestern*
the day after tomorrow	übermorgen	*œbermorgen*
this week	diese Woche	*deez-uh voKH-uh*
last week	letzte Woche	*letst-uh voKH-uh*
next week	nächste Woche	*nayKHst-uh voKH-uh*
this morning	heute morgen	*hoyt-uh morgen*
this afternoon	heute nachmittag	*hoyt-uh naKHmittahk*
this evening	heute abend	*hoyt-uh ahbent*
tonight	heute abend	*hoyt-uh ahbent*
yesterday afternoon	gestern nachmittag	*gestern naKHmittahk*
last night	gestern abend	*gestern ahbent*
tomorow morning	morgen früh	*morgen frœ*
tomorrow night	morgen abend	*morgen ahbent*
in three days	in drei Tagen	*in dry tahgen*
three days ago	vor drei Tagen	*for dry tahgen*
late	spät	*shpayt*
early	früh	*frœ*
soon	bald	*balt*
later on	später	*shpayter*
at the moment	im Moment	*im mohment*
second	die Sekunde	*zekoond-uh*
minute	die Minute	*minOOt-uh*
ten minutes	zehn Minuten	*tsayne minOOten*
quarter of an hour	eine Viertelstunde	*feertel-shtoond-uh*
half an hour	eine halbe Stunde	*halb-uh-shtoond-uh*
three quarters of an hour	eine dreiviertel Stunde	*ine-uh dry-feer-tel-shtoond-uh*
hour	die Stunde	*shtoond-uh*
day	der Tag	*tahk*

15

TIME

week	die Woche	*voKH-uh*
fortnight, 2 weeks	zwei Wochen	*tsvye voKH-en*
month	der Monat	*mohnat*
year	das Jahr	*yah*

TELLING THE TIME

Note how one says 'half to' the hour instead of 'half past'. Also the 24 hour clock is used much more commonly than in Britain and the USA, both in the written form as in timetables, and verbally as in enquiry offices and when making appointments.

one o'clock	ein Uhr	*ine OOr*
ten past one	zehn nach eins	*tsayne naKH eynss*
quarter past one	viertel nach eins	*feertel naKH eynss*
half past one	halb zwei	*halp tsvye*
twenty to two	zwanzig vor zwei	*tsvantsiKH for tsvye*
quarter to two	viertel vor zwei	*feertel for tsvye*
ten to two	zehn vor zwei	*tsayne for tsvye*
two o'clock	zwei Uhr	*tsvye OOr*
13.00 (1 pm)	dreizehn Uhr	*drytsayne OOr*
16.30 (4.30 pm)	sechzehn Uhr dreißig	*seKHtsayne OOr drysiKH*
20.10 (8.10 pm)	zwanzig Uhr zehn	*tsvansiKH OOr tsayne*
at half past five	um halb sechs	*oom halp zeks*
at seven o'clock	um sieben Uhr	*oom zeeben OOr*
noon	Mittag	*mittahk*
midnight	Mitternacht	*mitternaHKt*

HOTELS

Whether you want luxurious 4-star Hotel accommodation or simple bed-and-breakfast in a Pension, Gasthof or Gasthaus, you should find that each establishment displays a notice of the range of rooms available together with their prices.

USEFUL WORDS AND PHRASES

balcony	der Balkon	*balkong*
bathroom	das Bad	*baht*
bed	das Bett	*bet*
bedroom	das Schlafzimmer	*shlahf-tsimmer*
bill	die Rechnung	*reKHnoong*
breakfast	das Frühstück	*frœshtœk*
dining room	der Speiseraum	*shpyz-uh-rowm*
dinner	das Abendessen	*ahbent-essen*
double room	das Doppelzimmer	*doppel-tsimmer*
foyer	das Foyer	*foyay*
full board	Vollpension	*foll-pangzyohn*
half board	Halbpension	*halp-pangzyohn*
hotel	das Hotel	*hotel*
key	der Schlüssel	*shlœsel*
lift, elevator	der Fahrstuhl	*far-shtool*
lounge	der Gesellschaftsraum	*guzelshafts-rowm*
lunch	das Mittagessen	*mittak-essen*
manager	der Geschäftsführer	*gushefts-fœrer*
receipt	die Quittung	*kvittoong*
reception	der Empfang,	*empfang*
	die Rezeption	*raytsepts-yohn*
receptionist	der Portier,	*port-yay*
	die Empfangsdame (lady)	*empfangs-dahm-uh*
restaurant	das Restaurant	*restorant*
room	das Zimmer	*tsimmer*
room service	der Zimmerservice	*tsimmer-service*
shower	die Dusche	*doosh-uh*

single room	das Einzelzimmer	*ine-tsell-tsimmer*
toilet	die Toilette	*twalett-uh*
twin room	das Zweibettzimmer	*tsvy-bet-tsimmer*

Have you any vacancies?
Haben Sie Zimmer frei?
ha-ben zee tsimmer fry

I have a reservation
Ich habe ein Zimmer reserviert
iKH ha-buh ine tsimmer rezerveert

I'd like a single room
Ich möchte ein Einzelzimmer
iKH merKHt-uh ine ine-tsell-tsimmer

We'd like a double room
Wir möchten ein Doppelzimmer
veer merKHt-en ine doppeltsimmer

Do you have a twin room?
Haben Sie ein Zweibettzimmer?
ha-ben zee ine tsvye-bet-tsimmer

I'd like a room with a bathroom/balcony
Ich möchte ein Zimmer mit Bad/Balkon
iKH merKHt-uh ine tsimmer mit baht/balkong

I'd like a room for one night/three nights
Ich möchte ein Zimmer für eine Nacht/drei Nächte
iKH merKHt-uh ine tsimmer foor ine-uh naKHt/dry neKHt-uh

What is the charge per night?
Was kostet es pro Nacht?
vas kostet ess pro naKHt

REPLIES YOU MAY BE GIVEN

Tut mir leid, wir sind voll belegt
I'm sorry, we're full

Wir haben keine Doppelzimmer mehr frei
We have no double rooms left

Könnten Sie bitte im voraus bezahlen?
Please pay in advance

Sie müssen das Zimmer bis ... verlassen
Please vacate the room by ...

I don't know yet how long I'll stay
Ich weiß noch nicht, wie lange ich bleiben werde
iKH vice noKH niKHt vee lang-uh iKH blyben vaird-uh

When is breakfast/dinner?
Wann wird das Frühstück/Abendessen serviert?
van veert das frœshtook/ahbent-essen zair-veert

Would you have my luggage brought up
Können Sie mein Gepäck auf mein Zimmer bringen lassen?
kernen zee mine gupeck owf mine tsimmer bringen lassen

Please call me at ... o'clock
Bitte wecken Sie mich um ... Uhr
bitt-uh vecken zee miKH oom ... OOr

Can I have breakfast in my room?
Können Sie mir das Frühstück auf mein Zimmer bringen?
kernen zee meer das frœshtook owf mine tsimmer bringen

I'll be back at … o'clock
Ich bin um … Uhr wieder da
iKH bin oom … OOr veeder da

My room number is…
Meine Zimmernummer ist…
mine-uh tsimmer-noomer ist

I'm leaving tomorrow
Ich werde morgen abreisen
iKH vaird-uh morgen apryzen

May I have my bill please?
Kann ich bitte meine Rechnung haben?
kan iKH bitt-uh mine-uh reKHnoong ha-ben

Can you recommend another hotel?
Können Sie ein anderes Hotel empfehlen?
kernen zee ine anduhres hotel empfaylen

Can you get me a taxi?
Können Sie mir ein Taxi bestellen?
kernen zee meer ine taxi bushtell-en

THINGS YOU'LL SEE OR HEAR

Abendessen	dinner
Aufzug	lift, elevator
Bad	bath
Balkon	balcony
Doppelzimmer	double room
drücken	push
Dusche	shower
Einbettzimmer	single room
Einzelzimmer	single room
Empfang	reception
Erdgeschoß	ground floor
Fahrstuhl	elevator, lift
Frühstück	breakfast
Gepäck	luggage
Halbpension	half board
Kinder	children
Mehrwertsteuer	VAT
Mittagessen	lunch
Nacht	night
Notausgang	emergency exit
Rechnung	bill
Reservierung	reservation
Speisesaal	dining room
Stock	floor, storey
Toilette	toilet
Übernachtung	overnight stay
Übernachtung mit Frühstück	bed and breakfast
voll belegt	no vacancies
Vollpension	full board
ziehen	pull
Zimmer	room
Zimmer frei	vacancies
Zuschlag	supplement
Zweibettzimmer	twin room

CAMPING & CARAVANNING

The Federal Republic has over 1100 well-equipped campsites, most of which are open from May until September, while in some winter sports areas you will find sites open all year round.

In addition there are more than 650 youth hostels throughout the country, and mountain shelters provided by hiking clubs who also mark the more interesting trails.

USEFUL WORDS AND PHRASES

bucket	der Eimer	*eye-mer*
campsite	der Campingplatz	*kemping-plats*
campfire	das Lagerfeuer	*lager-foy-uh*
to go camping	Zelten gehen	*tselten gay-en*
caravan, R.V.	der Wohnwagen	*vohn-vahgen*
caravan site	der Wohnwagenplatz	*vohn-vahgen-plats*
cooking utensils	die Kochgeräte	*koKH-gurate-uh*
drinking water	das Trinkwasser	*trinkvasser*
ground sheet	die Zeltbodenplane	*tseltbohden-plahn-uh*
guy rope	die Zeltschnur	*tselt-shnOOr*
to hitch-hike	trampen	*trempen*
rope	das Seil	*zyle*
rubbish	der Abfall	*apfal*
rucksack	der Rucksack	*rookzack*
saucepans	die Kochtöpfe	*koKH-terpf-uh*
sleeping bag	der Schlafsack	*shlahfzack*
tent	das Zelt	*tselt*
youth hostel	die Jugendherberge	*yOOgent-hare-bairg-uh*

Can I camp here?
Kann man hier zelten?
kan man here tselten

Can we park the caravan (trailer) here?
Können wir den Wohnwagen hier abstellen?
kernen vere dane vohn-vahgen here apshtellen

Where is the nearest campsite/caravan site?
Wo ist der nächste Campingplatz/Campingplatz für Wohnwagen?
vo ist dare nayyKH-stuh kemping-plats/kemping-plats foor vohn-vahgen

What is the charge per night?
Was kostet es pro Nacht?
vas kostet ess pro naKHt

What facilities are there?
Welche Einrichtungen stehen zur Verfügung?
velKH-uh ine-riKHtoongen shtayen tsOOr fare-foogoong

Can I light a fire here?
Kann man hier ein Feuer machen?
kan man here ine foy-uh maKHen

Where can I get...?
Wo bekomme ich...?
vo bukomm-uh iKH

Is there drinking water here?
Gibt es hier Trinkwasser?
gipt ess here trinkvasser

THINGS YOU'LL SEE OR HEAR

Anhänger	trailer
Ausweis	pass, permit, identification
Benutzung	use
Campingplatz	campsite
Decke	blanket
Dusche	shower
Feuer	fire
Gebühren	charges
Hering	tent peg
Herbergsvater	youth hostel warden
Jugendherberge	youth hostel
Küche	kitchen
Leihgebühr	hire charge
leihen	to lend, borrow
Licht	light
offenes Feuer	open fire
Schlafraum	dormitory
Schlafsack	sleeping bag
Toilette	toilet
Trinkwasser	drinking water
Wohnwagen	caravan, trailer (R.V.)
Zelt	tent
Zelten verboten	no camping
Zeltpflock	tent peg
Zeltplane	tarpaulin
Zeltplatz	campsite
Zeltstange	tent pole

MOTORING

Drive on the right, overtake on the left. On dual-lane highways you may remain in the left-hand lane if there is dense traffic on your right, but when columns have formed in all lanes you are allowed to drive faster in a right-hand lane. If you happen to be in a left-hand lane you may move to the right only in order to turn off, stop, or follow directional arrows.

Traffic coming from the right has priority at crossroads and junctions wherever there is no priority sign or traffic light, unless entering the main road from a car park, service station, private road, path or forest track. Your right of way is signalled by a yellow diamond or the more familiar arrow inside a red triangle. The former gives you priority for some distance ahead while the latter is for the next intersection only. An inverted red triangle or an octagonal STOP sign denotes that you must give way.

In built-up areas a speed limit of 50 km/h (31 mph) is shown by the town's name on a yellow plate. The same plate with a diagonal red stripe marks the end of both limit and area. On other roads, except dual-lane highways, there is a speed limit of 100 km/h (62 mph). Heavier vehicles – trucks or lorries, buses, cars towing caravans or trailers – are restricted to 80 km/h (50 mph) on all roads and autobahns. There is no speed limit on the autobahns for automobiles.

For travel to West Berlin all foreign nationals require a passport. Motorists must also obtain a transit visa which will be issued at the control points on the GDR (East German) frontier and does not need to be applied for in advance.

SOME COMMON ROAD SIGNS

Baustelle	roadworks
Achtung! Straßenbahn	caution! Tramway
Ausfahrt	exit
Autobahnkreuz	motorway junction
Bei Frost Glatteisgefahr	icy in cold weather

→

Befolgen Sie die Parkverbote	please observe the "No Parking" signs
Eingeschränktes Halteverbot	no waiting
Ende der Autobahn	end of motorway
Freie Fahrt	no speed limit
Bahnübergang	level crossing
Einbahnstraße	one way street
Fahrradweg	cycle path
Frostschäden	frost damage
Fußgängerzone	pedestrian precinct
Gefährliche Einmündung	dangerous junction
Gefährliche Kurve	dangerous curve
Gegenverkehr	two-way traffic
Gegenverkehr hat Vorfahrt	oncoming traffic has right of way
Gesperrt für Fahrzeuge aller Art	closed to all vehicles
Glatteis	black ice
Halteverbot	no stopping
Höchstgeschwindigkeit	top/maximum speed
Langsam fahren	drive slowly
Nicht überholen	no overtaking
Nur für Anlieger	entry to adjacent premises only
Parkplatz	car park
Parkverbot	no parking
Radweg kreuzt	cycle track crossing
Raststätte	services
Sackgasse	no through road
Schlechte Fahrbahn	bad road
Starkes Gefälle	steep gradient
Steinschlag	falling rock
Überholen verboten	overtaking prohibited
Umleitung	diversion
Unebenheiten	rough road
Verengte Fahrbahn	road narrows

USEFUL WORDS AND PHRASES

boot	der Kofferraum	*koffer-rowm*
brake	die Bremse	*bremz-uh*
breakdown	die Panne	*pan-uh*
car	das Auto	*owtoh*
caravan	der Wohnwagen	*vone-vahgen*
crossroads	die Kreuzung	*kroytsoong*
to drive	fahren	*far-en*
engine	der Motor	*motohr*
exhaust	der Auspuff	*ows-poof*
fanbelt	der Keilriemen	*kyle-reemen*
garage (*for repairs*)	die Werkstatt	*vairkshtatt*
(*for fuel*)	die Tankstelle	*tankshtell-uh*
gasoline	das Benzin	*bentseen*
gear	der Gang	*gang*
gears	das Getriebe	*getreeb-uh*
junction		
(on motorway)	die Abfahrt	*apfahrt*
licence	der Führerschein	*fører-shine*
lights (*head*)	die Scheinwerfer	*shine-vairfer*
(*rear*)	die Rücklichter	*røk-liKHter*
lorry	der Lastwagen	*lasst-vahgen*
mirror	der Spiegel	*shpeegel*
motorbike	das Motorrad	*motohr-rat*
motorway	die Autobahn	*owtohbahn*
number plate	das Nummernschild	*noomern-shilt*
petrol	das Benzin	*bentseen*
road	die Straße	*shtras-uh*
skid	das Schleudern	*shloydern*
spares	die Ersatzteile	*airsats-tile-uh*
speed	die Geschwindigkeit	*gushvindiKH-kite*
speed limit	die Geschwindig-	*gushvindiKH-kites*
	keitsbeschränkung	*-bushrenkoong*
speedometer	der Tachometer	*taKHomayter*
steering wheel	das Lenkrad	*lenkrat*
tire, tyre	der Reifen	*rife-en*

to tow (away)	abschleppen	*apshleppen*
traffic lights	die Ampel	*ample*
trailer	der Anhänger	*anhenger*
trailer (R.V.)	der Wohnwagen	*vone-vahgen*
truck	der Lastwagen	*lasst-vahgen*
trunk	der Kofferraum	*koffer-rowm*
van	der Lieferwagen	*leefer-vahgen*
wheel	das Rad	*rat*
windscreen, windshield	die Windschutz-scheibe	*vintshoots -shybe-uh*

I'd like some fuel/oil/water
Ich brauche etwas Benzin/Öl/Wasser
iKH browKH-uh etvas bentseen/erl/vasser

Fill her up please!
Volltanken bitte!
folltanken bitt-uh

I'd like 10 litres of fuel
Zehn Liter Benzin bitte
tsayn leeter bentseen bitt-uh

Would you check the tires/tyres please?
Können Sie bitte die Reifen überprüfen?
kernen zee bitt-uh dee rife-en œber-prœfen

Where is the nearest garage?
Wo ist die nächste Werkstatt/Tankstelle?
vo ist dee nayKH-stuh vairkshtatt/tankshtell-uh

How do I get to...?
Wie komme ich nach...?
vee komm-uh iKH naKH

Is this the road to...?
Ist dies die Straße nach...?
ist deess dee shtras-uh naKH

DIRECTIONS YOU MAY BE GIVEN

geradeaus	straight on
links	left
links abbiegen	turn left
rechts	right
rechts abbiegen	turn right
erste Straße rechts	first on the right
zweite Straße links	second on the left
an dem/der ... vorbei	go past the...

Do you do repairs?
Machen Sie auch Reparaturen?
maKHen zee owKH reparatOOren

Can you repair the clutch?
Können Sie die Kupplung reparieren?
kernen zee dee kooploong repareeren

How long will it take?
Wie lange wird das dauern?
vee lang-uh veert das dow-ern

There is something wrong with the engine
Mit dem Motor stimmt etwas nicht
mit dame motohr shtimmt etvas niKHt

The engine is overheating
Der Motor ist heißgelaufen
dare motohr ist hice-gullowfen

MOTORING

The brakes are slipping
Die Bremsen sind zu lose
dee bremzen zint tsOO lohz-uh

I need a new tire/tyre
Ich brauche einen neuen Reifen
iKH browKH-uh ine-en noyen rife-en

I'd like to hire a car
Ich möchte ein Auto mieten
iKh merKHt-uh ine owtoh meeten

Where can I park?
Wo kann ich parken?
vo kan iKH parken

Can I park here?
Kann ich hier parken?
kan iKH here parken

THINGS YOU'LL SEE OR HEAR

Abfahrt	exit
Ausfahrt	exit
Autobahn	motorway
Autobahndreieck	motorway junction
Autobahnkreuz	motorway junction
Benzin	petrol, fuel
Bundesautobahn	federal motorway
Bundesstraße	federal highway
Gas geben	to accelerate
Kriechspur	crawler lane
Landstraße	country road
Luftdruck	air pressure
Münztank	coin-operated pump
Normal	2/3 star
Öl	oil
Ölstand	oil level
Reifendruck	tire/tyre pressure
reparieren	to repair
Reservetank	spare tank
Scheibenwischer	windscreen/shield wiper
Schlange	tailback
Seitenstreifen	hard shoulder
Stau	traffic jam
Super	4 star
Tankstelle	fuel/petrol station
überprüfen	to check
Umgehungsstraße	by-pass
Umleitung	diversion
Verkehrsdurchsage	traffic report
Verkehrsstockung	traffic hold-up
Wasser	water
Werkstatt	garage
Windschutzscheibe	windscreen, windshield
Zapfsäule	petrol pump

RAIL TRAVEL

The German Federal Railways are outstanding for their punctuality
and general efficiency. International trains connect Germany with
most parts of Europe, while fast, regular Inter-City and express trains
link the larger German towns and cities. The main types of train are:

TEE	Trans European Express
IC	Inter-City
D	Express
E	Semi-fast train
Personenzug	Stopping train, local train

A supplement (Zuschlag) is payable for all journeys by TEE and IC
trains and on D trains for journeys under 50kms.

USEFUL WORDS AND PHRASES

booking office	der Fahrkartenschalter	*farkarten-shalter*
buffet	das Büfett	*bew-fay*
carriage, car	der Wagen	*vah-gen*
compartment	das Abteil	*aptile*
connection	die Verbindung	*fare-bin-doong*
currency exchange	die Wechselstube	*vecksel-shtOOb-uh*
dining car	der Speisewagen	*shpyz-uh-vah-gen*
emergency cord	die Notbremse	*note-bremz-uh*
engine	die Lokomotive	*lokomoteev-uh*
entrance	der Eingang	*ine-gang*
exit	der Ausgang	*ows-gang*
first class	die erste Klasse	*airst-uh klass-uh*
to get in	einsteigen	*ine-shty-gen*
to get out	aussteigen	*ows-shty-gen*
guard	der Schaffner	*shaffner*
indicator board	die Anzeigetafel	*antsyg-uh-tahfel*

left luggage	die Gepäck-aufbewahrung	*gupeck-owf-bu-vahroong*
lost property	Fundsachen	*foont zaKHen*
luggage locker	das Gepäck-schließfach	*gupeck-shlees-faKH*
luggage rack	die Gepäckablage	*gupeck-ap-lahg-uh*
luggage trolley	der Kofferkuli	*koffer-kOOli*
luggage van	der Gepäckwagen	*gupeck-vah-gen*
platform	der Bahnsteig	*bahn-shtyke*
rail	das Gleis	*glice*
railway	die Eisenbahn	*eye-zen-bahn*
reserved seat	ein reservierter Platz	*ine rezer-veerter plats*
restaurant car	der Speisewagen	*shpy-zuh vah-gen*
return ticket	die Rückfahrkarte	*r0k-farkart-uh*
seat	der Platz	*plats*
second class	die zweite Klasse	*tsvyte-uh class-uh*
single ticket	die einfache Fahrkarte	*ine-faKH-uh farkart-uh*
sleeping car	der Schlafwagen	*shlahf-vahgen*
station	der Bahnhof	*bahn-hohf*
station master	der Bahnhofsvorsteher	*bahn-hohfs-forshtayer*
taxi	das Taxi	*taxi*
ticket	die Fahrkarte	*farkart-uh*
ticket collector	der Schaffner	*shaffner*
timetable	der Fahrplan	*far-plahn*
tracks	die Gleise	*glyz-uh*
train	der Zug	*tsOOk*
waiting room	der Wartesaal	*var-tuh-zahl*
window	das Fenster	*fenster*

When does the train for ... leave?
Wann fährt der Zug nach ... ab?
van fairt dare tsOOk naKH ... ap

When does the train from ... arrive?
Wann kommt der Zug aus ... an?
van komt dare tsOOk ows ... an

When is the next/first/last train to...?
Wann fährt der nächste/erste/letzte Zug nach...?
van fairt dare nayKH-stuh/air-stuh/let-stuh tsOOk naKH

What is the fare to...?
Was kostet eine Fahrt nach...?
vas kosstet ine-uh fart naKH

Do I have to change?
Muß ich umsteigen?
mooss iKH oomshtygen

Does the train stop at...?
Hält der Zug in...?
helt dare tsOOk in

How long does it take to get to...?
Wie lange dauert die Fahrt nach...?
vee lang-uh dow-ert dee fart naKH

A single/return ticket to ... please
Eine einfache Fahrkarte/eine Rückfahrkarte nach ... bitte
ine-uh ine-faKH-uh farkart-uh ine-uh rook-farkart-uh naKH ... bitt-uh

Do I have to pay a supplement?
Muß ich einen Zuschlag zahlen?
mooss iKH ine-en tsOO-shlahk tsahlen

I'd like to reserve a seat
Ich möchte gern einen Platz reservieren
ikh merKHt-uh gairn ine-en plats rezerveeren

REPLIES YOU MAY BE GIVEN

Es gibt nur Plätze erster Klasse
There are only 1st class seats

Sie müssen einen Zuschlag bezahlen
You must pay a supplement

Der nächste Zug fährt um...
The next train is at...

Der Zug hat Verspätung
The train is late

Sie müssen in ... umsteigen
You have to change at...

Is this the right train for...?
Ist dies der Zug nach...?
ist deess dare tsOOk naKH

Is this the right platform for the ... train?
Ist dies das Gleis für den Zug nach...?
ist deess das glice fœr dane tsOOk naKH

Which platform for the ... train?
Von welchem Gleis fährt der Zug nach...?
fon velKH-em glice fairt dare tsOOk naKH

Is the train late?
Hat der Zug Verspätung?
hat dare tsOOk fairshpay-toong

Could you help me with my luggage please?
Könnten Sie mir bitte mit meinem Gepäck behilflich sein?
kernten zee meer bitt-uh mit mine-em gupeck buhilf-liKH zine

Is this a non-smoking compartment?
Ist dies ein Nichtraucherabteil?
ist deess ine niKHt-rowKHer-aptile

Is this seat free?
Ist dieser Platz frei?
ist deezer plats fry

This seat is taken
Dieser Platz ist besetzt
deezer plats ist buzetst

I have reserved this seat
Ich habe eine Reservierung für diesen Platz
iKH ha-buh ine-uh rezerveer-oong fűr deezen plats

May I open/close the window?
Kann ich das Fenster öffnen/schließen?
kan iKH dass fenster erfnen/shleessen

When do we arrive in...?
Wann kommen wir in ... an?
van kommen veer in ... an

What station is this?
Welche Station ist dies?
velKH-uh shtatsyohn ist deess

When does my connection leave...?
Wann fährt mein Anschlußzug von ... ab?
van fairt mine anshloos-tsOOk fon ... ap

Do we stop at...?
Halten wir in...?
hal-ten veer in

Would you keep an eye on my things for a moment?
Könnten Sie bitte einen Moment auf meine Sachen aufpassen?
kernten zee bitt-uh ine-en mohment owf mine-uh zaKHen owfpassen

Is there a restaurant car on this train?
Hat dieser Zug einen Speisewagen?
hat deezer tsOOk ine-en shpyze-uh-vahgen

THINGS YOU'LL SEE OR HEAR

Abfahrt	departure(s)
Achtung	attention
Ankunft	arrival(s)
Auskunft	information
aussteigen	to get out
Ausstieg	exit
Bahnhof	station
Bahnhofsmission	help for needy travellers
Bahnhofspolizei	railway police
Bahnsteig	platform
Bahnsteigkante	edge of the platform
Bahnsteigkarte	platform ticket
besetzt	engaged
bitte von der Bahnsteig-kante zurücktreten	stand clear of the platform edge
Einfahrt	arrival
einsteigen	to get in
Einsteigen und Türen schließen	please close the doors
Einstieg	entry
Fahrkarten	tickets
Fahrkartenautomat	ticket machine
Fahrplan	timetable
Fahrt	journey
Feiertag	holiday
frei	vacant
Gepäckaufbewahrung	left luggage
Gepäckschließfächer	luggage lockers
Gleis	platform
hält nicht in...	does not stop in...
Hauptbahnhof (Hbf)	central station
Imbiß	snacks
kein Ausstieg	no exit
kein Einstieg	no entry

Mißbrauch strafbar	penalty for misuse
nicht hinauslehnen	do not lean out
Nichtraucher	non-smokers
Notbremse	emergency cord
planmäßig	scheduled
Platzkarte	seat reservation
Rauchen verboten	no smoking
Raucher	smokers
Reiseauskunft	travel information
reserviert	reserved
samstags	Saturdays
Schnellzug	express
Schnellzugzuschlag	express train supplement
sonnabends	Saturdays
sonn- und feiertags	Sundays and holidays
Schlafwagen	sleeping car
Speisewagen	restaurant car
Strecke	route
Wagenstandanzeiger	order of cars
Toilette	toilet
verkehrt nicht an...	... days excepted
verkehrt nur an...	... days only
Verspätung	delay
Vorsicht bei der Einfahrt des Zuges!	warning to stand clear of arriving train
Wagen	carriage, car
Wartesaal	waiting room
Wechselstube	currency exchange
zu den Zügen	to the trains
Zug fährt sofort ab!	train is ready to leave
zurücktreten	to stand back, to stand clear
Zuschlag	supplement

AIR TRAVEL

In addition to an excellent domestic network, air services connect the following West German cities with many UK and USA destinations: West Berlin, Bremen, Cologne (Köln)/Bonn, Düsseldorf, Frankfurt am Main, Hamburg, Hanover, Munich (München), Nuremberg (Nürnberg) and Stuttgart.

USEFUL WORDS AND PHRASES

aircraft	das Flugzeug	flook-tsoyk
air hostess	die Stewardess	stewardess
airline	die Fluglinie	flook-leenyuh
airport	der Flughafen	flook-ha-fen
airport bus	der Flughafenbus	flook-ha-fen-booss
aisle	der Mittelgang	mittle-gang
arrival	die Ankunft	ankoonft
baggage claim	die Gepäckausgabe	gupeck-ows-gahb-uh
boarding card	eine Bordkarte	bort-kartuh
check-in	die Abfertigung	ap-fare-tee-goong
check-in desk	der Abfertigungs-schalter	ap-fare-tee-goongs-shalter
delay	die Verzögerung	fare-tserg-uh-roong
departure	der Abflug	ap-flook
departure lounge	die Abflughalle	apflook-hal-uh
emergency exit	der Notausstieg	note-ows-shteek
flight	der Flug	flook
flight number	die Flugnummer	flook-noomer
gate	der Flugsteig	flook-shtyke
jet	das Düsenflugzeug	dwzen-flook-tsoyk
	der Jet	jet
land	landen	landen
passport	der Paß	pas
passport control	die Paßkontrolle	pas-kontroll-uh
pilot	der Pilot	pil-oht
runway	die Startbahn	shtart-bahn

seat	der Platz	*plats*
seat belt	der Gurt	*goort*
steward	der Steward	*steward*
stewardess	die Stewardess	*stewardess*
take off	abheben	*ap-hayben*
window	das Fenster	*fenster*
wing	die Tragfläche	*trahk-fleKH-uh*

When is there a flight to...?
Wann geht ein Flug nach...?
van gate ine flook naKH

What time does the flight to ... leave?
Wann geht das Flugzeug nach...?
van gate das flook-tsoyk naKH

Is it a direct flight?
Gibt es einen Direktflug?
gipt es ine-en deerekt-flook

Do I have to change planes?
Muß ich umsteigen?
moos iKH oom-shty-gen

When do I have to check-in?
Wann ist die Abfertigung?
van ist dee apfare-tee-goong

I'd like a single/return ticket to...
Einen enfachen Flug/einen Rückflug nach ... bitte
ine-en ine-faKHen flook/ine-en rook-flook naKH ... bitt-uh

I'd like a non-smoking seat please
Ich hätte gern einen Platz auf der Nichtraucherseite
ikh het-uh gairn ine-en plats owf dare niKHt-rowKHer zyte-uh

I'd like a window seat please
Ich hätte gern einen Fensterplatz
iKH het-uh gairn ine-en fenster plats

How long will the flight be delayed?
Wie lange wird die Verzögerung dauern?
vee lang-uh veert dee fare-tserg-uh roong dowern

Is this the right gate for the ... flight?
Ist dies der Flugsteig für die Maschine nach...
ist dees dare flOOk-shtyke fʊr dee masheen-uh naKH

When do we arrive in...?
Wann kommen wir in ... an?
van kommen veer in ... an

May I smoke now?
Kann ich jetzt rauchen?
kan iKH yetst rowKHen

I do not feel very well
Ich fühle mich nicht sehr gut
ikh fʊl-uh miKH niKHt zare gOOt

THINGS YOU'LL SEE OR HEAR

Abfertigung	check-in
Abflug	departure(s)
Ankunft	arrival(s)
Auskunft	information
bitte anschnallen	fasten seat belts
Direktflug	direct flight
einchecken	to check in
Flug	flight
Flugdauer	flight time
Fluggäste	passengers
Fluggeschwindigkeit	flight speed
Flughöhe	altitude
Flugkapitän	captain
Flugsteig	gate
Gangway	steps
Gepäckausgabe	baggage claim
Gepäckkontrolle	baggage control
Handgepäck	hand luggage
Landung	landing
Linienflug	scheduled flight
Maschine	aircraft
Nichtraucher	non-smokers
Notausstieg	emergency exit
Notlandung	emergency landing
Ortszeit	local time
Passagiere	passengers
Paßkontrolle	passport control
Rauchen einstellen	refrain from smoking
Rauchen verboten	no smoking
Raucher	smokers
startbereit	ready for take-off
Verspätung	delay
Verzögerung	delay
Zwischenlandung	intermediate stop

LOCAL TRANSPORT, BOAT TRAVEL

There is a good bus and tram (streetcar) network in all German towns and cities. Single tickets can be bought from the driver, but it is usually cheaper to buy a multi-journey ticket from ticket machines or tobacconists. The ticket has to be stamped when boarding and you may change en route without having to buy a new ticket.

Some of the larger cities such as Hamburg, Munich, Berlin, Frankfurt, Cologne and Nuremburg have an underground or subway system (U-Bahn) and some cities also have a fast local rail system (S-Bahn). Zone systems also operate in major cities, a flat fare applying in each zone with the fare increasing according to the number of zones crossed. Tickets can be obtained from automatic ticket machines, most of which will give change.

A number of rural bus services are also run by the German Federal Railways and Federal Post. Post buses are yellow, while those belonging to the Federal Railways are red.

A more leisurely way of travelling in Germany, especially during the summer months, is on one of the steamer services operated on the major rivers such as the Rhine, Mosel and Danube and on Lake Constance, the Bavarian lakes and the Berlin lakes.

USEFUL WORDS AND PHRASES

adult	der Erwachsene	*airvax-en-uh*
boat	das Schiff	*shiff*
bus	der Bus	*booss*
bus stop	die Bushaltestelle	*booss-hal-tuh-shtell-uh*
child	das Kind	*kint*
coach	der Bus	*booss*
conductor	der Schaffner	*shaffner*
connection	die Verbindung	*fare-bindoong*
cruise	die Kreuzfahrt	*kroyts-fart*

downstream	flußabwarts	*flooss-ap-vairts*
driver	der Fahrer	*far-uh*
fare	der Fahrpreis	*far-price*
ferry	die Fähre	*fare-ruh*
lake	der See	*zay*
network map	eine Verkehrsnetz-Übersichtskarte	*fare-cares nets œber-siKHts-kart-uh*
number 5 bus	die Buslinie 5	*booss-leenyuh*
passenger	der Passagier	*passa-jeer*
port	der Hafen	*ha-fen*
quay	der Kai	*kye*
river	der Fluß	*flooss*
sea	das Meer	*mare*
seat	der Platz	*plats*
ship	das Schiff	*shiff*
station	der Bahnhof	*bahn-hohf*
taxi	das Taxi	*taxi*
terminus	die Endstation	*ent-shtatsyohn*
ticket	eine Fahrkarte	*farkart-uh*
tram, streetcar	die Straßenbahn	*shtrahssen-bahn*
tram stop	die Straßenbahn-haltestelle	*shtrahssen-bahn-hal-tuh-shtell-uh*
tube, subway	die U-Bahn	*OO-bahn*
upstream	flußaufwärts	*flooss-owf-vairts*

Where is the nearest underground station?
Wo ist die nächste U-Bahn-Station?
vo ist dee nayKHst-uh OO-bahn shtatsyohn

Where is the bus station?
Wo ist der Busbahnhof?
vo ist dare booss-bahnhohf

Where is there a bus stop/tram stop?
Wo ist eine Bushaltestelle/eine Straßenbahnhaltestelle?
vo ist ine-uh booss-hal-tuh-shtell-uh/ine-uh shtrahssen-bahn-hal-tuh-shtell-uh

Which buses go to...?
Welche Busse fahren nach...?
velKH-uh booss-uh far-en nakh

How often do the buses/trams to ... run?
Wie oft verkehren die Busse/Bahnen nach...?
vee oft fare-care-ren dee booss-uh/bahn-en naKH

Would you tell me when we get to...?
Können Sie mir sagen, wann wir in ... ankommen?
kernen zee mere zah-gen van veer in ... an-kommen

Do I have to get off yet?
Muß ich hier aussteigen?
mooss iKH here ows-shtygen

How do you get to...?
Wie fährt man am besten nach...?
vee fairt man am besten naKH

Is it very far?
Ist es weit von hier?
ist ess vite fon here

I want to go to...
Ich möchte nach ... fahren
iKH merKHt-uh naKH ... far-en

Do you go near...?
Fahren Sie in die Nähe von...?
far-en zee in dee nay-uh fon

Where can I buy a ticket?
Wo kann ich eine Fahrkarte lösen?
vo kan iKH ine-uh farkart-uh lerzen

Please open/close the window
Könnten Sie bitte das Fenster öffnen/schließen?
kernten zee bitt-uh das fenster erfnen/shleessen

Could you help me get a ticket?
Könnten Sie mir bitte helfen, eine Fahrkarte zu lösen?
kernten zee mere bitt-uh helfen ine-uh farkart-uh tsOO lerzen

When does the last bus leave?
Wann fährt der letzte Bus?
van fairt dare letste booss

Where can I get a taxi?
Wo kann ich ein Taxi bekommen?
vo kan iKH ine taxi bukkommen

Stop here, please
Halten Sie bitte hier
halten zee bitt-uh here

I'd like a receipt
Ich hätte gern eine Quittung
iKH hett-uh gairn ine-uh kvittoong

THINGS YOU'LL SEE OR HEAR

Abfahrt	departure
abgezähltes Geld	exact fare
Ankunft	arrival
Ausstieg	exit
Ausweis	pass
Automat	machine
Behinderte	handicapped persons
bezahlen	to pay
einfach	single
einfache Fahrt	single journey
Einstieg	entry
Einstieg vorn/hinten	entry at front/rear
einwerfen	to insert
Endstation	terminus
Entwerter	stamping machine

→

47

Erwachsene	adults
Fahrer	driver
Fahrkarte	ticket
Fahrkartenautomat	ticket machine
Fahrkartenkontrolle	ticket inspection
Fahrschein	ticket
Geldeinwurf	insert coins
Geldrückgabe	returned coins
Gleis	track
Hafenrundfahrt	boat trip round the harbour
Haltestelle	stop
kein Einstieg	no entry
Kinder	children
Kontrolleur	inspector
Kurzstrecke	short journey
Linie	route
Monatskarte	monthly ticket
Münzen	coins
Netzkarte	travelcard
Notausstieg	emergency exit
Notbremse	emergency brake
Rauchen verboten	no smoking
Rückfahrkarte	return ticket
Sammelkarte	multi-journey ticket
S-Bahn	local railway system
Sitzplätze	seats
Station	stop
Stehplätze	standing room
Straßenbahn	tram
Tageskarte	day ticket
U-Bahn	underground, tube, subway
U-Bahnhof	underground station
umsteigen	to change
vorzeigen	to show
Wochenkarte	weekly ticket

RESTAURANT

USEFUL WORDS AND PHRASES

beer	das Bier	*beer*
bill	die Rechnung	*reKHnoong*
bottle	die Flasche	*flash-uh*
bowl	die Schüssel	*shœsel*
butter	die Butter	*bootter*
cake	der Kuchen	*kOOKHen*
chef	der Chefkoch	*shef-koKH*
coffee	der Kaffee	*kaffay*
cup	die Tasse	*tass-uh*
glass	das Glas	*glahss*
fork	die Gabel	*gah-bel*
knife	das Messer	*messer*
menu	die Speisekarte	*shpyze-uh-kart-uh*
milk	die Milch	*milKH*
plate	der Teller	*teller*
receipt	die Quittung	*kvittoong*
sandwich	ein belegtes Brötchen	*bullayktess brertKHen*
serviette	die Serviette	*zair-vee-ett-uh*
snack	der Imbiß	*imbiss*
soup	die Suppe	*zoop-uh*
spoon	der Löffel	*lerfel*
sugar	der Zucker	*tsooker*
table	der Tisch	*tish*
tea	der Tee	*tay*
teaspoon	der Teelöffel	*tay-lerfel*
tip	das Trinkgeld	*trink-gelt*
waiter	der Ober	*ober*
waitress	die Bedienung	*budeen-oong*
water	das Wasser	*vasser*
wine	der Wein	*vine*
wine list	die Weinkarte	*vinekart-uh*

A table for 2 please
Einen Tisch für zwei Personen bitte
ine-en tisch für tsvye pair-zonen bitt-uh

I'd like to reserve a table for 8 o'clock
Ich möchte gern einen Tisch für 20 Uhr reservieren
iKH merKHt-uh gairn ine-en tish für tsvantsiKH OOr rezervee ren

Can we see the menu?
Könnten wir bitte die Speisekarte haben?
kernten veer bitt-uh dee shpyze-uh-kart-uh ha-ben

Can we see the wine list?
Könnten wir die Weinkarte haben?
kernten veer dee vinekart-uh ha-ben

What would you recommend?
Was können Sie empfehlen?
vas kernen zee empfay-len

I'd like...
Ich hätte gern...
iKH het-uh gairn

I only want a snack
Ich möchte nur einen Imbiß
iKH merKHt-uh nOOr ine-en imbiss

I just want a cup of coffee/tea
Ich möchte nur eine Tasse Kaffee/Tee
iKH merKHt-uh nOOr ine-uh tass-uh kaffay/tay

Is there a set menu?
Gibt es ein Tagesgericht?
gipt ess ine tahgess-guriKHt

May we have some more...?
Können wir noch etwas ... haben?
kernen veer noKH etvas ... hahben

50

I didn't order this
Das habe ich nicht bestellt
das hahb-uh iKH niKHt bushtellt

Waiter!/Waitress!
Herr Ober!/Fräulein!
hair ober/froy-line

Can I have another knife please?
Kann ich bitte ein anderes Messer haben?
kan iKH bitt-uh ine ander-es messer ha-ben

Can we have the bill please?
Können wir bitte die Rechnung haben?
kernen veer bitt-uh dee reKHnoong ha-ben

We'll pay together/separately
Wir bezahlen zusammen/getrennt
veer butsahlen tsOOzammen/gutrennt

I think there's a mistake in the bill
Ich glaube, in der Rechnung ist ein Fehler
iKH glowb-uh in dare reKHnoong ist ine fayler

I'd like a receipt
Ich hätte gern eine Quittung
iKH hett-uh gairn ine-uh kvittoong

The meal was very good, thank you
Das Essen war sehr gut, vielen Dank
das essen var zair gOOt feelen dank

My compliments to the chef!
Sprechen Sie dem Koch meinen Glückwunsch aus!
shpreKHen zee dame koKH mine-en glOOkvoonsh owss

Aal	eel
Aalsuppe	eel soup
am Spieß	on the spit
Ananas	pineapple
Apfel	apple
Apfel im Schlafrock	baked apples in puff pastry
Apfelkompott	stewed apples
Apfelmus	apple purée
Apfelsaft	apple juice
Apfelsine	orange
Apfelstrudel	apple strudel
Apfeltasche	apple turnover
Apfelwein	cider
Aprikose	apricot
Artischocken	artichokes
Aspik	aspic
Auberginen	aubergines
Auflauf	(baked) pudding or omelette
Aufschnitt	sliced cold cuts
Austern	oysters
Avocado	avocado
Backobst	dried fruit
Backpflaume	prune
Baiser	meringue
Balkansalat	cabbage and pepper salad
Banane	banana
Bandnudeln	ribbon noodles
Basilikum	basil
Bauernauflauf	bacon and potato omelette
Bauernfrühstück	bacon and potato omelette
Bauernomelett	bacon and potato omelette
Bechamelkartoffeln	sliced potatoes in creamy sauce
Bechamelsauce	creamy sauce with onions and ham
Bedienung	service
Beilage	side dish
Berliner	jam doughnut
Bier	beer
Birnen	pears
Biskuit	sponge
Biskuitrolle	Swiss roll

Bismarckhering	filleted pickled herring
Blätterteig	puff pastry
blau	au bleu
Blumenkohl	cauliflower
blutig	rare
Blutwurst	blood sausage
Bockwurst	large frankfurter
Bohnen	beans
Bohneneintopf	bean stew
Bohnensalat	bean salad
Bohnensuppe	bean soup
Bouillon	clear soup
Braten	roast meat
Bratensoße	gravy
Brathering	(pickled) fried herring (*served cold*)
Bratkartoffeln	fried potatoes
Bratwurst	grilled pork sausage
Broccoli	broccoli
Brot	bread
Brust	breast
Brötchen	roll
Brühwurst	large frankfurter
Bückling	smoked red herring
bunt	mixed
Buttercremetorte	cream cake
Buttermilch	buttermilk
Champignons	mushrooms
Champignonsauce	mushroom sauce
Chicoree	chickory
Chinakohl	Chinese cabbage
Cordon bleu	veal cordon bleu
Currywurst	curried pork sausage
Deutsches Beefsteak	mince patty
Dicke Bohnen	broad beans
Dill	dill
durchgebraten	well-done
durchwachsen	with fat
durchwachsener Speck	streaky bacon
Eier	eggs
Eierauflauf	omelette
Eierkuchen	pancake
Eierpfannkuchen	pancake

Eierspeise	egg dish
eingelegt	pickled
Eintopf	stew
Eintopfgericht	stew
Eis	ice
Eisbecher	sundae
Eisbein	knuckles of pork
Eissplittertorte	ice chip cake
Endiviensalat	endive salad
englisch	(*of meat*) rare
Entenbraten	roast duck
entgrätet	boned
Erbsen	peas
Erbsensuppe	pea soup
Erdbeertorte	strawberry cake
Essig	vinegar
Falscher Hase	meat loaf
Fasan	pheasant
Feldsalat	lamb's lettuce
Fenchel	fennel
Fett	fat
Filet	fillet (steak)
Fisch	fish
Fischfilet	fish fillet
Fischfrikadelle	fishcake
Fischstäbchen	fish fingers
flambiert	flambéd
Fleischbrühe	bouillon
Fleischkäse	meat loaf
Fleischklößchen	meat ball(s)
Fleischpastete	meat vol-au-vent
Fleischsalat	diced meat salad with mayonnaise
Fleischwurst	pork sausage
Fond	meat juices
Forelle	trout
Forelle blau	trout au bleu
Forelle Müllerin (Art)	trout with butter and lemon (breaded)
Frikadelle	rissole
Frikassee	fricassee
fritiert	(deep-)fried
Froschschenkel	frog's legs
Fruchtsaft	fruit juice

Frühlingsrolle	spring roll
Gabelrollmops	rolled-up pickled herring, rollmops
Gans	goose
Gänsebraten	roast goose
Gänseleber	goose liver
Gänseleberpastete	goose liver pâté
garniert	garnished
Gebäck	pastries, cakes
gebacken	fried
gebeizt	marinaded
gebraten	roast
gebunden	thickened
gedünstet	steamed
Geflügel	poultry
Geflügelleber	chicken liver
Geflügelleberragout	chicken liver ragout
gefüllt	stuffed
gefüllte Kalbsbrust	veal roll
gegart	cooked
gekocht	boiled
gekochter Schinken	boiled ham
Gelee	jelly
Gemüse	vegetable(s)
Gemüseplatte	assorted vegetables
Gemüsesalat	vegetable salad
Gemüsesuppe	vegetable soup
gepökelt	salted, pickled
geräuchert	smoked
Gericht	dish
geschmort	braised/stewed
Geschnetzeltes	strips of meat in thick sauce
Geselchtes	salted and smoked meat
gespickt	larded
Getränke	beverages
Gewürz	spice
Gewürzgurken	gherkins
Goldbarsch	type of perch
gratiniert	au gratin
Grieß	semolina
Grießklößchen	semolina dumplings
Grießpudding	semolina pudding
Grießsuppe	semolina soup

grüne Bohnen	French beans
grüne Nudeln	green pasta
grüner Aal	fresh eel
Grünkohl	(curly) kale
Gulasch	goulash
Gulaschsuppe	goulash soup
Gurkensalat	cucumber salad
Hackfleisch	mince
Hähnchen	chicken
Hähnchenkeule	chicken leg
Haifischflossensuppe	shark-fin soup
Hammelbraten	roast mutton
Hammelfleisch	mutton
Hammelkeule	leg of mutton
Hammelrücken	saddle of mutton
Hartkäse	hard cheese
Haschee	hash
Hasenkeule	haunch of hare
Hasenpfeffer	jugged hare
Hauptspeise	main course
Hausfrauenart	home-made-style
Hausmacher (Art)	home-made-style
Hecht	pike
Heidelbeeren	blueberries
Heilbutt	halibut
Heringssalat	herring salad
Heringsstipp	herring salad
Heringstopf	pickled herrings
Herz	heart
Herzragout	heart ragout
Himbeeren	raspberries
Himmel und Erde	potato and apple purée with blood and liver sausage
Hirn	brains
Hirschbraten	roast venison
Hirschmedaillons	small venison fillets
Honig	honey
Honigkuchen	honeycake
Honigmelone	honey melon
Hüfte	haunch
Hühnerbrühe	chicken broth

Hühnerfrikassee	chicken fricassée
Hühnersuppe	chicken soup
Hülsenfrüchte	peas and beans
Hummer	lobster
Jägerschnitzel	pork with mushrooms
Kabeljau	cod
Kaffee	coffee
Kaiserschmarren	sugared pancake with raisins
Kakao	cocoa
Kalbfleisch	veal
Kalbsbraten	roast veal
Kalbsbries	sweetbread
Kalbsfrikassee	veal fricassée
Kalbshaxe	leg of veal
Kalbsmedaillons	small veal fillets
Kalbsnierenbraten	roast veal with kidney
Kalbsschnitzel	veal cutlet
Kalte Platte	cold meal
Kalter Braten	cold meat
Kaltes Büfett	cold buffet
Kaltschale	cold sweet soup
Kaninchen	rabbit
Kaninchenbraten	roast rabbit
Kapern	capers
Karamelpudding	caramel pudding
Karotten	carrots
Karpfen	carp
Kartoffelbrei	potato purée
Kartoffelklöße	potato dumplings
Kartoffelknödel	potato dumplings
Kartoffeln	potatoes
Kartoffelpuffer	potato fritters
Kartoffelpüree	potato purée
Kartoffelsalat	potato salad
Kartoffelsuppe	potato soup
Käse	cheese
Käse-Sahne-Torte	cream cheesecake
Käsegebäck	cheese savouries
Käsekuchen	cheesecake
Käseplatte	selection of cheeses
Käsesalat	cheese salad
Käsesauce	cheese sauce

Käsespätzle	home-made noodles with cheese
Kasserolle	casserole
Kassler	smoked and braised pork chop
Kastanien	chestnuts
Keule	leg, *(of game)* haunch
Kirschen	cherries
klare Brühe	clear soup
Klöße	dumplings
Knäckebrot	crispbread
Knacker	frankfurter
Knackwurst	frankfurter
Knoblauch	garlic
Knoblauchbrot	garlic bread
Knochen	bone
Knochenschinken	ham on the bone
Knödel	dumplings
Kognak	brandy
Kohl	cabbage
Kohlrabi	kohlrabi
Kompott	stewed fruit
Konfitüre	jam
Königinpastete	chicken vol-au-vent
Königsberger Klopse	meatballs in caper sauce
Königskuchen	type of fruit cake
Kopfsalat	lettuce
Kotelett	chop
Krabben	shrimps/prawns
Krabbencocktail	prawn cocktail
Kräuter	herbs
Kräuterbutter	herb butter
Kräuterkäse	cheese flavoured with herbs
Kräuterquark	curd cheese with herbs
Kräutersauce	herb sauce
Kräutertee	herbal tea
Krautsalat	coleslaw
Krebs	crayfish
Kresse	cress
Kroketten	croquettes
Kruste	crust
Kuchen	cake
Kürbis	pumpkin
Labskaus	meat, fish and potato stew

Lachs	salmon
Lachsersatz	sliced and salted pollack
Lachsforelle	sea trout
Lachsschinken	smoked rolled fillet of ham
Lamm	lamb
Lammrücken	saddle of lamb
Lauch	leek
Leber	liver
Leberkäse	baked pork and beef loaf
Leberklöße	liver dumplings
Leberknödel	liver dumplings
Leberpastete	liver pate
Leberwurst	liver sausage
Leipziger Allerlei	mixed vegetables
Likör	liqueur
Limonade	lemonade
Linseneintopf	lentil stew
Linsensuppe	lentil soup
mager	lean
Majoran	marjoram
Makrele	mackerel
Makrone	macaroon
Mandeln	almonds
Marinade	marinade
Mariniert	marinaded, pickled
Markklößchen	marrow dumplings
Marmelade	jam
Marmorkuchen	marble cake
Maronen	sweet chestnuts
Matjes(hering)	young herring
Medaillons	small fillets
Meeresfisch	seafish
Meeresfrüchte	seafood
Meerrettich	horseradish
Meerrettichsauce	horseradish sauce
Mehlspeise	sweet dish, flummery
Mehrwertsteuer	value added tax, VAT
Melone	melon
Miesmuscheln	mussels
Milch	milk
Milchmixgetränk	milk shake
Milchreis	rice pudding

Mineralwasser	(sparkling) mineral water
Mohnkuchen	poppyseed cake
Möhren	carrots
Mohrrüben	carrots
Most	fruit wine
Mus	purée
Muscheln	mussels
Muskat(nuß)	nutmeg
MwSt = Mehrwertsteuer	VAT
Nachspeise	dessert
Nachtisch	dessert
Napfkuchen	ring-shaped poundcake
natürlich	natural
Nieren	kidneys
Nudeln	pasta
Nudelsalat	noodle salad
Nudelsuppe	noodle soup
Nüsse	nuts
Obstsalat	fruit salad
Ochsenschwanzsuppe	oxtail soup
Öl	oil
Oliven	olives
Olivenöl	olive oil
Omelett	omelette
Orange	orange
Orangensaft	orange juice
Palatschinken	stuffed pancakes
paniert	with breadcrumbs
Paprika	peppers
Paprikasalat	pepper salad
Paprikaschoten	peppers
Parmesankäse	parmesan cheese
Pastete	vol-au-vent
Pellkartoffeln	potatoes boiled in their jackets
Petersilie	parsley
Petersilienkartoffeln	potatoes with parsley
Pfannkuchen	pancake
Pfeffer	pepper
Pfifferlinge	chanterelles
Pfirsich	peach
Pflaume	plum
Pflaumenkuchen	plum tart

Pflaumenmus	plum jam
Pichelsteiner Topf	vegetable stew with diced beef
pikant	spicy
Pikkolo	quarter bottle of champagne
Pilze	mushrooms
Platte	selection
pochiert	poached
Pökelfleisch	salt meat
Pommes frites	French fried potatoes
Porree	leek
Potthast	braised beef with sauce
Poularde	young chicken
Preiselbeeren	cranberries
Preßkopf	brawn
Prinzeßbohnen	unsliced runner beans
Pumpernickel	black rye bread
Püree	(potato) purée
püriert	pureed
Putenschenkel	turkey leg
Puter	turkey
Quark	curd cheese
Quarkspeise	curd cheese dish
Radieschen	radishes
Rahm	(sour) cream
Räucheraal	smoked eel
Räucherhering	kipper, smoked herring
Räucherlachs	smoked salmon
Räucherspeck	smoked bacon
Rauchfleisch	smoked meat
Rehbraten	roast venison
Rehgulasch	venison goulash
Rehkeule	haunch of venison
Rehrücken	saddle of venison
Reibekuchen	potato waffles
Reis	rice
Reisauflauf	rice pudding
Reisbrei	creamed rice
Reissalat	rice salad
Remoulade	remoulade
Renke	whitefish
Rettich	radish
Rhabarber	rhubarb

Rinderschmorbraten	pot roast
Rinderzunge	ox tongue
Rindfleisch	beef
Rindfleischsalat	beef salad
Rindfleischsuppe	beef broth
Rippchen	sparerib
roh	raw
Rohkostplatte	selection of salads
Rollmops	rolled-up pickled herring, rollmops
rosa	rare to medium
Rosenkohl	Brussels sprouts
Rosinen	raisins
Rostbraten	roast
Rostbratwurst	barbecued sausage
Röstkartoffeln	fried potatoes
Rotbarsch	type of perch
Rote Bete	beetroot
rote Grütze	red fruit jelly
Rotkohl	red cabbage
Rotwein	red wine
Rührei	scrambled eggs
Rumpsteak	rump steak
Russische Eier	egg mayonnaise
Sahne	cream
Sahnesauce	cream sauce
Sahnetorte	cream gateau
Salat	salad
Salatplatte	selection of salads
Salatsauce	salad dressing
Salz	salt
Salzhering	salted herring
Salzkartoffeln	boiled potatoes
Salzkruste	salty crusted skin
Sandkuchen	type of Madeira cake
sauer	sour
Sauerbraten	marinated potroast
Sauerkraut	white cabbage finely chopped and pickled

Sauerrahm	sour cream
Schaschlik	(shish-) kebab
Schattenmorellen	morello cherries
Schellfisch	haddock
Schildkrötensuppe	real turtle soup
Schillerlocken	smoked haddock rolls
Schinken	ham
Schinkenröllchen	rolled ham
Schinkenwurst	ham sausage
Schlagsahne	whipped cream
Schlei	tench
Schmorbraten	pot roast
Schnecken	snails
Schnittlauch	chives
Schnitzel	cutlet
Schokolade	chocolate
Scholle	plaice
Schulterstück	piece of shoulder
Schwarzbrot	brown rye bread
Schwarzwälder Kirschtorte	Black Forest cherry gateau
Schwarzwurzeln	salsifies
Schweinebauch	belly of pork
Schweinbraten	roast pork
Schweinefilet	fillet of pork
Schweinefleisch	pork
Schweinekotelett	pork chop
Schweineleber	pig's liver
Schweinerippe	cured pork chop
Schweinerollbraten	rolled roast of pork
Schweineschmorbraten	roast pork
Schweineschnitzel	pork fillet
Schweinshaxe	knuckle of pork
Seelachs	pollack
Seezunge	sole
Sekt	sparkling wine, champagne
Sellerie	celery
Selleriesalat	celery salad
Semmelknödel	bread dumplings
Senf	mustard
Senfsahnesauce	mustard and cream sauce
Senfsauce	mustard sauce
Serbisches Reisfleisch	diced pork, onions, tomatoes, rice

Soleier	pickled eggs
Soße	sauce, gravy
Soufflé	soufflé
Spanferkel	suckling pig
Spargel	asparagus
Spargelcremesuppe	cream of asparagus
Spätzle	home-made noodles
Speck	bacon
Speckknödel	bacon dumplings
Specksauce	bacon sauce
Speisekarte	menu
Spiegeleier	fried eggs
Spießbraten	joint roasted on a spit
Spinat	spinach
Spitzkohl	white cabbage
Sprudel(wasser)	mineral water
Stachelbeeren	gooseberries
Stangen(weiß) brot	French bread
Steak	steak
Steinpilze	type of mushroom
Streuselkuchen	sponge cake with crumble topping
Suppe	soup
Suppengrün	mixed herbs and vegetables (in soup)
Szegediner Gulasch	goulash with pickled cabbage
Sülze	brawn
süß	sweet
süß-sauer	sweet-and-sour
Süßwasserfisch	freshwater fish
Tafelwasser	(still) mineral water
Tafelwein	table wine
Tatar	steak tartare
Taube	pigeon
Tee	tea
Teigmantel	pastry covering
Thunfisch	tuna
Tintenfisch	squid
Tomaten	tomatoes
Tomatensalat	tomato salad
Tomatensuppe	tomato soup
Törtchen	tart(s)
Torte	gateau
Truthahn	turkey

überbacken	au gratin
Ungarischer Gulasch	Hungarian Goulash
Ungebraten	unfried
Vanille	vanilla
Vanillesauce	vanilla sauce
verlorene Eier	poached eggs
Vollkornbrot	dark rye bread
vom Grill	grilled
vom Rost	grilled
Vorspeise	hors d'oeuvre, starter
Waffeln	waffles
Waldorfsalat	salad with celery, apples and walnuts
Wasser	water
Wassermelone	water melon
Weichkäse	soft cheese
Weinbergschnecken	snails
Weinbrand	brandy
Weincreme	pudding with wine
Weinsauce	wine sauce
Weinschaumcreme	creamed pudding with wine
Weintrauben	grapes
Weißbrot	white bread
Weißkohl	white cabbage
Weißkraut	white cabbage
Weißwein	white wine
Wiener Schnitzel	veal in breadcrumbs
Wild	game
Wildschweinkeule	haunch of wild boar
Wildschweinsteak	wild boar steak
Windbeutel	cream puff
Wirsing	savoy cabbage
Wurst	sausage
Wurstplatte	selection of sausages
Wurstsalat	sausage salad
Würstchen	frankfurter(s)
würzig	spicy
Zander	pike-perch, zander
Zigeunerschnitzel	pork with peppers and relishes
Zitrone	lemon
Zitronencreme	lemon cream
Zucchini	courgettes
Zucker	sugar

Zuckererbsen	mange-tout peas
Zunge	tongue
Zungenragout	tongue ragout
Zutaten	ingredients
Zwiebeln	onions
Zwiebelringe	onion rings
Zwiebelsuppe	onion soup
Zwiebeltorte	onion tart
Zwischengericht	entrée

SHOPPING

Shops in Germany are generally open from 9 am to 6.30 pm, except on Saturdays when they close at 2 pm. However, on the first Saturday of each month most shops remain open until 6 pm.

USEFUL WORDS AND PHRASES

audio equipment	Phonoartikel	*fono-arteekle*
baker	der Bäcker	*becker*
boutique	die Boutique	*boutique*
butcher	der Metzger	*metsger*
	der Fleischer	*flysher*
bookshop	die Buchhandlung	*bOOKH-handloong*
to buy	kaufen	*kowfen*
cake shop	die Konditorei	*kondee-toreye*
cheap	billig	*billiKH*
chemist	die Apotheke	*appotake-uh*
department store	das Kaufhaus	*kowf-house*
fashion	Mode	*moh-duh*
faulty	fehlerhaft	*fayler-haft*
fishmonger	das Fischgeschäft	*fish-gusheft*
grocer	das Lebensmittel-geschäft	*laybens-mittel-gusheft*
ironmonger	die Eisenwaren-handlung	*eyzen-vahren-handloong*
ladies' wear	Damenbekleidung	*dahmen-buklydoong*
menswear	Herrenbekleidung	*herren-buklydoong*
newsagent	der Zeitungshändler	*tsyte-oongs-hendler*
off-licence, liquor store	die Wein- und Spirituosenhandlung	*vine oont shpirit-oo-ohzen-handloong*
pharmacy	die Apotheke	*appotake-uh*
receipt	die Quittung	*kvittoong*

record shop	das Schallplatten- geschäft	*shallplatten-gusheft*
sale	der Schlußverkauf	*shloos-fare-kowf*
shoe shop	das Schuhgeschäft	*shOO-gusheft*
shop	das Geschäft	*gusheft*
to go shopping	einkaufen gehen	*ine-kowfen gay-en*
souvenir shop	der Andenkenladen	*andenken-lahden*
special offer	das Sonderangebot	*zonder-an-gubote*
to spend	ausgeben	*owss-gayben*
stationer	die Schreibwaren- handlung	*shrype-vahren -handloong*
supermarket	der Supermarkt	*zOOpermarkt*
tailor	der Schneider	*shnyder*
take-away	der Schnellimbiß	*shnell-imbiss*
till	die Kasse	*kass-uh*
travel agent	das Reisebüro	*ryze-uh-bœroh*
toyshop	die Spielwaren- handlung	*shpeelvahren -handloong*

I'd like...
Ich hätte gern...
iKH het-uh gairn

Do you have...?
Haben Sie...?
ha-ben zee

How much is this?
Was kostet das?
vas kostet das

Do you have any more of these?
Haben Sie noch mehr hiervon?
ha-ben zee noKH mare here-fon

Have you anything cheaper?
Haben Sie etwas Billigeres?
ha-ben zee etvas billiger-es

Have you anything larger?
Haben Sie etwas Größeres?
ha-ben zee etvas grersuh-res

Have you anything smaller?
Haben Sie etwas Kleineres?
ha-ben zee etvas kline-uh-res

Does it come in other colours?
Gibt es das in anderen Farben?
gipt es das in anderen far-ben

Can I try it/them on?
Kann ich es/sie anprobieren?
kan iKH ess/zee anprobeer-en

Where do I pay?
Wo kann ich bezahlen?
vo kan iKH butsahlen

I'd like to change this please
Ich möchte dies gerne umtauschen
iKH merKHt-uh dees gairn-uh oomtowshen

Can I have a refund?
Kann ich mein Geld zurückbekommen?
kan iKH mine gelt tsOOrœck-bukommen

REPLIES YOU MAY BE GIVEN

Kann ich Ihnen behilflich sein?
Can I help you?

Möchten Sie es anprobieren?
Would you like to try it on?

Das haben wir leider nicht vorrätig
I'm sorry, we're out of stock

Ein Umtausch gegen bar ist nicht möglich
We cannot give cash refunds

Ich kann Ihnen eine Gutschrift geben
I can give you a credit note

Das ist alles was wir haben
That is all we have

Haben Sie es etwas kleiner?
Have you any smaller money?

Tut mir leid, den Schein kann ich nicht wechseln
Sorry, I've no change for that note

I'm just looking
Ich sehe mich nur um
iKH zay-uh miKH nOOr oom

I'll come back later
Ich komme später noch einmal wieder
iKH komm-uh shpayter noKH ine-mahl veeder

Where is the ... department?
Wo ist die ... -Abteilung?
vo ist dee ... -aptile-oong

Can I have a receipt?
Kann ich bitte eine Quittung haben?
kan iKH bitt-uh ine-uh kvittoong ha-ben

Could you wrap it for me?
Können Sie es bitte einwickeln?
kernen zee ess bitt-uh ine-vickeln

Can I have a bag please?
Kann ich bitte eine Tüte haben?
kan iKH bitt-uh ine-uh tœt-uh ha-ben

THINGS YOU'LL SEE OR HEAR

Abteilung	department
Anzahlung	deposit
Ausverkauf	sale
ausverkauft	sold out
Autovermietung	car hire
Bäckerei	bakery
billig	cheap
bitte klingeln	please ring (for service)
Blumen	flowers
Buchhandlung	bookshop
Büroartikel	office supplies
Damenbekleidung	ladies' clothes
Dutzend	dozen
Einkauf	purchase
Fleischerei	butcher's shop
frisch	fresh
Gemüse	vegetables
Getränke	drinks
halb	half
Heimwerkerbedarf	do-it-yourself supplies
herabgesetzt	reduced
Herrenbekleidung	menswear
Imbißstube	snack bar
Kaffee	coffee
Kaufhaus	department store
Kilo	kilogramme
Konditorei	cake shop
Lebensmittel	groceries
Metzgerei	butcher
Mode	fashion
Monatsraten	monthly instalments
Obergeschoß	upper floor
Obst	fruit

Pelze	furs
Pfund	pound
Phonoartikel	audio equipment
Preis	price
preisgünstig	inexpensive
preiswert	inexpensive
Qualität	quality
Raten	instalments
Reisebüro	travel agent
Schnellimbiß	snack bar
Schreibwaren	stationery
Schuhe	shoes
Selbstbedienung	self-service
Sommerschlußverkauf	summer sale
Sonderangebot	special offer
Sonderpreis	special price
Spielwaren	toys
Spirituosen	spirits
Spitzenqualität	high quality
Supermarkt	supermarket
Süßwaren	confectionery
Tabakwaren	tobacco supplies
Tee	tea
Teppiche	carpets
Umtausch nur gegen Quittung	goods are not exchanged without a receipt
vergriffen	unavailable, (*book*) out of print
Vermietung	rental
Waren	goods
Winterschlußverkauf	winter sale
Zeitschriften	magazines
Zeitungen	newspapers

AT THE HAIRDRESSER

It is useful to remember that most hairdressers in Germany do not open on Mondays.

USEFUL WORDS AND PHRASES

appointment	der Termin	*tare-meen*
beard	der Bart	*bart*
blond	blond	*blont*
brush	bürsten	*berst-en*
comb	kämmen	*kemm-en*
conditioner	der Haarfestiger	*hah-festiger*
curlers	Lockenwickler	*lockenvickler*
curling tongs	die Brennschere	*brenshare-uh*
curly	kraus	*krowss*
dark	dunkel	*doonkel*
fringe	der Pony	*ponnee*
gel	das Gel	*gayl*
hair	das Haar	*hah*
haircut	der Haarschnitt	*hah-shnitt*
hairdresser	der Friseur, der Frisör	*frizz-er*
hairdryer	der Fön	*fern*
(for ladies)	die Trockenhaube	*trocken-howb-uh*
highlights	Strähnchen	*shtrayn-KHen*
long	lang	*lang*
moustache	der Schnurrbart	*shnoorbart*
parting	der Scheitel	*shytle*
perm	die Dauerwelle	*dowervell-uh*
shampoo	das Shampoo	*shampoo*
shave	rasieren	*razeeren*
shaving foam	die Rasiercreme	*razeer-kraym*
short	kurz	*koorts*
styling mousse	der Festiger	*festiger*
wavy	wellig	*velliKH*

I'd like to make an appointment
Ich hätte gern einen Termin
ikh het-uh gairn ine-en tare-meen

Just a trim please
Nur etwas nachschneiden bitte
nOor etvas naKHshnyden bitt-uh

Not too much off
Bitte nicht zu kurz
bitt-uh niKHt tsOO koorts

A bit more off here please
Hier bitte etwas kürzer
here bitt-uh etvas kertser

I'd like a cut and blow-dry
Schneiden und fönen bitte
shnyden oont fernen bitt-uh

I'd like a perm
Ich möchte gern eine Dauerwelle
ikh merKHt-uh gairn ine-uh dowervell-uh

I'd like a shampoo and set
Waschen und legen bitte
vashen oont laygen bitt-uh

I'd like highlights
Ich hätte gern Strähnchen
ikh het-uh gairn shtrayn-KHen

THINGS YOU'LL SEE OR HEAR

Bart	beard
Coiffeur	hair stylist
Damensalon	ladies' salon
Dauerwelle	perm
Fassonschnitt	short back and sides
fönen	blow dry
Frisiersalon	hair dressing salon
Frisör	hairdresser
Haarstudio	hairdressing studio
Herrensalon	men's hairdresser
hinten	at the back
kurz	short
kürzer	shorter
legen	set
lang	long
Locken	curls
Nacken	back of the neck
Pony	fringe
rasieren	shave
Rasierklinge	razor blade
Rasierseife	shaving soap
Scheitel	parting
schneiden	cut
Seite	side
tönen	tint
trocknen	dry
vorn	at the front
waschen	wash
waschen und legen	wash and set

SPORTS

Whatever your sport and wherever you are in Germany you will find no lack of facilities. The many lakes and rivers as well as the North Sea and Baltic Sea coasts provide excellent opportunities for swimming, sailing, canoeing, fishing, sailboarding etc, while an extensive network of well-marked footpaths make Germany an ideal country for walking. Cycling too is popular and cycles can be hired almost everywhere, including at a large number of railway stations.

Germany is known throughout the world as a centre for winter sports with around 300 resorts, mainly concentrated in the Alps, Black Forest and Harz. In addition, many other areas have good facilities for cross-country skiing, while most of the larger towns have an ice-rink, often open all year round.

USEFUL WORDS AND PHRASES

Alps	die Alpen	*alpen*
athletics	Leichtathletik	*lyKHt-atlayteek*
badminton	Federball	*fayder-bal*
ball	der Ball	*bal*
beach	der Strand	*shtrant*
bicycle	das Fahrrad	*far-rat*
binding	die Bindung	*bin-doong*
blizzard	der Schneesturm	*shnay-shtoorm*
canoe	das Kanu	*kahn-OO*
cross-country-skiing	der Langlauf	*lang-lowf*
current	die Strömung	*shtrer-moong*
deckchair	der Liegestuhl	*leeg-uh-shtOOl*
to dive	tauchen	*towKHen*
diving board	das Sprungbrett	*shproong-brett*
fishing	das Angeln,	*ang-eln*
	das Fischen	*fishen*
fishing rod	die Angelrute	*ang-ell-rOOt-uh*

flippers	die Schwimmflossen	shvimm-flossen
football	Fußball	fOOss-bal
football match	das Fußballspiel	fOOss-bal-shpeel
golf	Golf	golf
golf course	der Golfplatz	golf-plats
gymnastics	Turnen	toor-nen
ice-hockey	Eishockey	ice-hockey
ice rink	das Eisstadion	ice-shtahdee-ohn
	die Eisbahn	ice-bahn
jogging	das Jogging	jogging
lake	der See	zay
lift pass	der Liftpaß	lift-pas
mountaineering	das Bergsteigen	bairk-shtygen
piste	die Piste	pist-uh
racket	der Schläger	shlayger
riding	Reiten	ryten
rowing boat	das Ruderboot	rOOder-boht
to run	laufen	lowfen
saddle	der Sattel	sattle
sailboard	das Windsurfbrett	vint-zurf-brett
sailing	Segeln	zaygeln
sand	der Sand	zant
sea	das Meer	mare
to ski	Ski fahren	shee far-en
ski boots	die Skistiefel	shee shteefel
ski lift	der Skilift	shee-lift
skis	die Skier	shee-uh
ski-trail	die Piste	pist-uh
to skate	Schlittschuh laufen	shlitshOO lowfen
skates	die Schlittschuhe	shlitshOO-uh
sledge	der Schlitten	shlitten
snorkel	der Schnorchel	shnorKHel
snow	der Schnee	shnay
stadium	das Stadion	shtahdee-on
to swim	schwimmen	shvimmen
swimming pool	das Schwimmbad	shvim-bat
tennis	Tennis	tennis

tennis court	der Tennisplatz	*tennis-plats*
tennis racket	der Tennisschläger	*tennis-shlayger*
tent	das Zelt	*tselt*
volleyball	Volleyball	*volley-bal*
walking	Wandern	*van-dern*
water skis	die Wasserskier	*vasser-shee-uh*
wave	die Welle	*vell-uh*
winter sports	der Wintersport	*vinter-shport*
yacht	die Jacht	*yaKHt*

How do I get to the beach?
Wie komme ich zum Strand?
vee komm-uh iKH tsoom shtrant

How deep is the water here?
Wie tief ist das Wasser hier?
vee teef ist das vasser here

Is there an indoor/outdoor pool here?
Gibt es hier ein Hallenbad/Freibad?
gipt ess here ine hal-en-bat/fry-bat

Is it safe to swim here?
Ist das Schwimmen hier ungefährlich?
ist das shvimmen here oon-gufare-liKH

Do I need a licence?
Braucht man eine Genehmigung?
browKHt man ine-uh gename-igoong

I would like to hire a bike
Ich möchte ein Fahrrad leihen
iKH merKHt-uh ine far-rat lye-en

How much does it cost per hour/day?
Wieviel kostet das pro Stunde/Tag?
veefeel kostet das pro shtoond-uh/tak

When does the lift start?
Wann geht der Lift?
van gate dare lift

How much is a daily/weekly lift pass?
Was kostet eine Tageskarte/Wochenkarte für den Lift?
vas kosstet ine-uh tahges-kart-uh/voKHen-kart-uh fœr dane lift

Where are the nursery slopes?
Wo sind die Anfängerhügel?
vo zint dee anfenger-hœgel

I would like to take skiing lessons
Ich möchte gern Skistunden nehmen
iKH merKHt-uh gairn shee-shtoonden naymen

Is it very steep?
Ist es sehr steil?
ist ess zair shtyle

Where can I hire...?
Wo kan ich ... leihen?
vo kann iKH ... lye-en

THINGS YOU'LL SEE OR HEAR

Angeln verboten	no fishing
Betreten der Eisfläche verboten	keep off the ice
Bootsverleih	boat hire
Eisstadion	ice rink
Erholungsgebiet	recreational area
Erste Hilfe	first aid
Fahrradvermietung	bicycle hire
Fahrradweg	cycle path
Freibad	open-air swimming pool
Fußgänger	pedestrians
Gefahr	danger
gefährliche Strömung	dangerous current
Hallenbad	indoor swimming pool
Langlauf	cross-country skiing
Lawinengefahr	danger avalanches
Loipe	ski-trail
Naturschutzgebiet	nature reserve
Radfahrer	cyclist
Reitweg	bridle path
Rodelbahn	toboggan run
Rudern	to row, rowing
Schneefall	snowfall
Schneesturm	blizzard
Schneeverwehung	snowdrift
Schwimmbad	swimming pool
Segeln	to sail, sailing
Skipiste	ski slope
Sprungschanze	ski jump
Tauchen	to dive, diving
Tauwetter	thaw
Wandern	to walk, walking
Windsurfen	windsurfing
zum Skilift	to the ski lift

POST OFFICE

There is usually at least one person with a knowledge of English in most Post Offices and therefore few difficulties should be encountered with transactions.

Letter boxes in Germany are yellow.

USEFUL WORDS AND PHRASES

airmail	Luftpost	*looft-posst*
collection	die Leerung	*lairroong*
counter	der Schalter	*shallter*
customs form	das Zollformular	*tsoll-formoolar*
delivery	die Zustellung	*tsOO-shtelloong*
deposit	die Spareinlage	*shpar-ine-lahg-uh*
form	das Formular	*formoolahr*
letter	der Brief	*breef*
letter box	der Briefkasten	*breef-kasten*
mail	die Post	*posst*
main post office	die Hauptpost	*howpt-posst*
money order	die Postanweisung	*posst-anvize-oong*
package	das Paket	*packate*
parcel	das Paket	*packate*
post	die Post	*posst*
postage rates	das Porto	*porto*
postal order	die Geldanweisung	*gelt-anvize-oong*
postcard	die Postkarte	*posstkart-uh*
postcode	die Postleitzahl	*posstlite-tsahl*
poste-restante	postlagernd	*posst-lagernt*
postman	der Briefträger	*breef-trayger*
post office	das Postamt	*posst-amt*
registered letter	das Einschreiben	*ine-shryben*
savings	das Sparguthaben	*shpargOOt-ha-ben*
stamp	die Briefmarke	*breef-mark-uh*

surface mail	Post auf dem Landweg	*owf dame lantvake*
telegram	das Telegramm	*telegram*
telephone	das Telefon	*telephone*
telephone box	die Telefonzelle	*telephone-tsell-uh*
withdrawal	die Abhebung	*ap-hay-boong*

How much is a letter to...?
Was ist das Porto für einen Brief nach...?
vas ist das porto foor ine-en breef naKH

What stamps do I need for a postcard to...?
Welche Marke brauche ich für eine Postkarte nach...?
velKH-uh mark-uh browKH-uh iKH foor ine-uh posstkart-uh naKH

I would like three 1 Mark stamps
Ich hätte gern drei Briefmarken zu einer Mark
iKH het-uh gairn dry breef-marken tsOO ine-er mark

I want to register this letter
Ich möchte diesen Brief als Einschreiben senden
iKH merKHt-uh deezen breef als ine-shryben zenden

I want to send this parcel to...
Ich möchte dieses Paket nach ... senden
iKH merKHt-uh deezes packate naKH ... zenden

How long does the post/mail to ... take?
Wie lange ist die Post nach ... unterwegs?
vee lang-uh ist dee posst naKH ... oonter-vayks

Where can I post/mail this?
Wo kann ich das aufgeben?
vo kan iKH das owf-gayben

Is there any mail for me?
Ist Post für mich da?
ist posst foor miKH dah

I'd like to send a telegram
Ich möchte ein Telegramm schicken
iKH merKHt-uh ine telegram shicken

This is to go airmail
Ich möchte dies mit Luftpost schicken
iKH merKHt-uh deess mit looft-posst shicken

THINGS YOU'LL SEE OR HEAR

Absender	sender
Adresse	address
ausfüllen	to fill in
Auslandsporto	postage to abroad
Beamte	official
Brief	letter
Briefmarke	stamp
Einschreibsendungen	registered mail
Einzahlungen	deposits
Empfänger	addressee
Fernsprecher	telephone
Gebühr	charge
geöffnet	open
geschlossen	closed
Hausnummer	number
Inlandsporto	inland postage
Luftpostsendungen	airmail
nächste Leerung ...	next collection
Öffnungszeiten	opening hours
Ort	place
Päckchen	packet, package

Paket	parcel
Paketannahme	parcels counter
Porto	postage
Postamt	post office
Postanweisungen	money order
Postkarte	postcard
postlagernde Sendungen	poste-restante
Postleitzahl	postcode
Postsparkasse	giro bank
Postwertzeichen	stamp
Postwertzeichen in kl. Mengen	stamps in small quantities
Schalter	counter
Straße	street
Telefonzelle	telephone box
Telegramme	telegrams

TELEPHONE

Telephone boxes in Germany are painted yellow and are of two types depending on the value of the coins which can be inserted. International calls can only be made from boxes that show a green disc with the word "Ausland" or "International". To telephone the UK, dial 0044 followed by the area code (but exclude the 0 which prefixes all UK area codes) and the number you want. To call a USA number, dial 1 followed by the area code and the subscriber's number.

The tones you'll hear when telephoning in Germany are:

Dialling tone	:	same as in UK and USA
Ringing	:	This is a 1-second burst of tone every four seconds.
Engaged	:	rapid pips similar to UK and USA
Unobtainable	:	voice says "Kein Anschluß unter dieser Nummer", and you'll hear 3 short pips of ascending pitch.

Depending on which type of box it is the following coins are used: 10pf, 50pf, 1 mark, 5 marks. Telephone numbers are always read out in pairs of numbers, ie 302106 is said "dreißig, einundzwanzig, null sechs" (thirty, twenty one, zero six).

USEFUL WORDS AND PHRASES

call	ein Anruf	*anrOOf*
to call	anrufen	*anrOOfen*
code	die Vorwahl	*for-vahl*
crossed line	die Fehlverbindung	*fale-farebindoong*
to dial	wählen	*vale-en*
dialling tone	das Amtszeichen	*amts-tsyKHen*
emergency	ein Notfall	*note-fal*
enquiries	Auskunft	*ows-koonft*

extension	der Nebenanschluß	*nayben-anshlooss*
international call	ein Auslandsgespräch	*ows-lants-gushprayKH*
number	die Nummer	*noom-uh*
operator	die Vermittlung	*fare-mittloong*
pay-phone	der Münzfernsprecher	*mœnts-fairn-shpreKHer*
push-button phone	das Tastentelefon	*tasten-telephone*
receiver	der Hörer	*her-uh*
reverse charge call	ein R-Gespräch	*air-gushprayKH*
ringing tone	das Freizeichen	*fry-tsyKHen*
telephone	das Telefon	*telephone*
telephone box	eine Telefonzelle	*telephone-tsell-uh*
telephone directory	das Telefonbuch	*telephone-bOOKH*
wrong number	die falsche Nummer	*falsh-uh noom-uh*

Where is the nearest phone box?
Wo ist die nächste Telefonzelle?
vo ist dee nayKHst-uh telephone-tsell-uh

Is there a telephone directory?
Gibt es ein Telefonbuch?
gipt ess ine telephone-bOOKH

I would like the directory for...
Ich hätte gern das Telefonbuch für...
iKH het-uh gairn das telephone-bOOKH fœr

I want to make an international call
Ich möchte ins Ausland anrufen
iKH merKHt-uh ins ows-lant anrOOfen

87

Can I call abroad from here?
Kann ich von hier ins Ausland telefonieren?
kan iKH fon here ins ows-lant telephone-eeren

How much is a call to...?
Was kostet ein Gespräch nach...?
vas kostet ine gushprayKH naKH

I would like to reverse the charges
Ich möchte ein R-Gespräch führen
iKH merKHt-uh ine air-gushprayKH fœren

I would like a number in...
Ich hätte gern eine Nummer in...
iKH het-uh gairn ine-uh noom-uh in

Hallo, this is ... speaking
Hallo, hier spricht...
hallo here shpriKHt...

Is that...?
Bin ich mit ... verbunden?
bin iKH mit ... fare-boonden

Speaking
Am Apparat
am appa-raht

I would like to speak to...
Kann ich bitte ... sprechen?
kan iKH bitt-uh ... shpreKHen

Extension ... please
Anschluß ... bitte
anshlooss ... bitt-uh

Please tell him ... called
Bitte sagen Sie ihm, ... hat angerufen
bitt-uh zah-gen zee eem ... hat angurOOfen

Ask him to call me back please
Bitte sagen Sie ihm, er möchte mich zurückrufen
bitt-uh zah-gen zee eem air merKHt-uh miKH tsOOroock-rOOfen

My number is...
Meine Nummer ist...
mine-uh noom-uh ist

Do you know where he is?
Wissen Sie, wo er ist?
vissen zee vo air ist

When will he be back?
Wann wird er zurück sein?
van veert air tsOOroock zine

Could you leave a message?
Können Sie ihm etwas ausrichten?
kernen zee eem etwas ows-riKHten

I'll ring back later
Ich rufe später zurück
iKH rOOf-uh shpayter tsOOroock

Sorry, wrong number
Tut mir leid, falsch verbunden
tOOt mere lite, falsh fare-boonden

The phone is out of order
Das Telefon ist kaputt
das telefone isst kapoott

Could you please connect me with this number?
Könnten Sie mich bitte mit dieser Nummer verbinden?
kernten zee miKH bitt-uh mit deezer noomer fairbinden

REPLIES YOU MAY BE GIVEN

Am Apparat.
Speaking.

Tut mir leid, er ist nicht im Hause
Sorry, he's not in

Wer spricht bitte?
Who's calling?

Wen möchten Sie sprechen?
Who do you want to speak to?

Kann er Sie zurückrufen?
Can he call you back?

Sie sind falsch verbunden
You've got the wrong number.

Er ist um ... zurück.
He'll be back at ...

Ich verbinde.
I'll put you through.

Kein Anschluß unter dieser Nummer
Number unobtainable

THINGS YOU'LL SEE OR HEAR

abnehmen	to lift (the receiver)
Apparat	telephone
Ausland	abroad
besetzt	engaged
defekt	out of order
Durchwahl	direct dialing
Einheit	unit
einwerfen	to insert
fasse dich kurz!	be brief!
Ferngespräch	long-distance call
Fernsprecher	telephone
Feuer	fire
Feuerwehr	fire brigade
Freizeichen	dialling tone
Gabel	hook
Gelbe Seiten	yellow pages
Gespräch	call, conversation
Hörer	receiver
Münzen	coins
Nebenanschluß	extension
Notruf	emergency call
örtlich	local
Ortsgespräch	local call
Rufnummer	number
Störungsstelle	faults service
Tarif	charges
Telefonbuch	telephone directory
Telefonzelle	telephone box
Vermittlung	operator
Vorwahl	dialling code
wählen	to dial
Wählscheibe	dial
warten	to wait

HEALTH

Under the EEC Social Security regulations visitors from the UK qualify for treatment on the same basis as the Germans themselves. You must complete the form CM1 (at your own Social Security office) a month at least before travelling. You then get a certificate (E111) for use if you need treatment, plus an explanatory leaflet.

In Germany all chemists' shops *(Apotheke)* are independent private concerns. There are no chainstore chemists like Boots in Britain. They sell exclusively medicines and a small assortment of drugstore goods which have some medicinal use. In every town you will find an *Apotheke* that is open all night or over the weekend. Those that are closed will display a notice showing which one is open, and the local newspaper also advertises the *"dienstbereit"* or "duty" chemist. The owner or an assistant pharmacist opens the door after you've rung the night bell.

In Germany there are two categories of medicines; those sold over the counter and those which can only be obtained on a doctor's prescription.

USEFUL WORDS AND PHRASES

accident	der Unfall	*oon-fal*
ambulance	der Krankenwagen	*kranken-vahgen*
anaemic	blutarm	*bloot-arm*
appendicitis	die Blinddarmentzün- dung	*blintdarm-ent -tsOOndoong*
appendix	der Blinddarm	*blintdarm*
aspirin	die Kopfschmerz- tablette	*kopfshmairts -tablette-uh*
asthma	das Asthma	*astma*
backache	Rückenschmerzen	*rœken-shmairtsen*
bandage	der Verband	*fairbant*
bite	der Biß	*biss*
(of insect)	der Stich	*shtiKH*

92

bladder	die Blase	*blahz-uh*
bleed	bluten	*blOOten*
blister	die Blase	*blahz-uh*
blood	das Blut	*blOOt*
blood donor	der Blutspender,	*blOOt-shpender*
	die Blutspenderin (f)	*blOOt-shpenderin*
burn	die Verbrennung	*fare-brenoong*
cancer	Krebs	*krayps*
catarrh	der Katarrh	*kattahr*
chemist	die Apotheke	*apo-take-uh*
chest	die Brust	*broost*
chickenpox	Windpocken	*vintpocken*
cold	die Erkältung	*airkeltoong*
concussion	die Gehirner-	*geheern-air*
	schütterung	*-shœtteroong*
constipation	die Verstopfung	*fare-shtopfoong*
contact lenses	Kontaktlinsen	*kontakt-linzen*
corn	das Hühnerauge	*hœner-owg-uh*
cough	der Husten	*hOOsten*
cut	der Schnitt	*shnitt*
dentist	der Zahnarzt	*tsahn-artst*
diabetes	die Zuckerkrankheit	*tsooker-krank-hite*
diarrhoea	der Durchfall	*doorKH-fal*
dizzy	schwindlig	*shvindliKH*
doctor	der Arzt	*artst*
earache	Ohrenschmerzen	*or-en-shmairtsen*
fever	das Fieber	*feeber*
filling	die Füllung	*fœl-oong*
first aid	Erste Hilfe	*airst-uh hilf-uh*
flu	die Grippe	*grip-uh*
fracture	der Bruch	*brooKH*
German measles	Röteln	*rerteln*
glasses	die Brille	*brill-uh*
haemorrhage	die Blutung	*blOOtoong*
hayfever	der Heuschnupfen	*hoyshnoopfen*
headache	Kopfschmerzen	*kopfshmairtsen*

heart	das Herz	*hairts*
heart attack	der Herzinfarkt	*hairts-infarkt*
hospital	das Krankenhaus	*kranken-house*
ill	krank	*krank*
indigestion	die Magenverstim-mung	*mahgen-fare-shtimm-oong*
inflammation	die Entzündung	*ent-tsœndoong*
injection	die Spritze	*shprits-uh*
injury	die Verletzung	*fare-letsoong*
itch	das Jucken	*yooken*
kidney	die Niere	*neer-uh*
lung	die Lunge	*loong-uh*
lump	der Knoten	*knoht-en*
measles	Masern	*mahzern*
migraine	die Migräne	*migray-nuh*
mumps	Mumps	*moomps*
nausea	die Übelkeit	*œbelkite*
nurse	die Krankenschwester	*krankenshvester*
ointment	die Salbe	*zalb-uh*
operation	die Operation	*operatsyohn*
optician	der Augenarzt	*owgen-artst*
pain	der Schmerz	*shmairts*
penicillin	Penizillin	*penitsileen*
pill	die Pille	*pill-uh*
plaster	das Pflaster	*pflaster*
pneumonia	die Lungenentzün-dung	*loongen-entsœn-doong*
pregnant	schwanger	*shvanger*
prescription	das Rezept	*raytsept*
rash	der Ausschlag	*ows-shlahk*
rheumatism	das Rheuma	*royma*
scald	die Verbrühung	*fare-brœ-oong*
scratch	der Kratzer	*kratser*
sling	die Schlinge	*shling-uh*
smallpox	Pocken	*pocken*
sore	eine wunde Stelle	*ine-uh voond-uh shtell-uh*

sore throat	Halsschmerzen	*hals-shmairtsen*
splinter	der Splitter	*shplitter*
sprain	die Verstauchung	*fare-shtowKHoong*
sting	der Stich	*shtiKH*
stomach	der Magen	*mahgen*
	der Bauch	*bowKH*
sunstroke	der Sonnenstich	*zonnen-shtiKH*
tablet	die Tablette	*tablet-uh*
temperature	das Fieber	*feeber*
throat	die Kehle	*kayl-uh*
tonsils	die Mandeln	*mandeln*
tooth	der Zahn	*tsahn*
toothache	Zahnschmerzen	*tsahn-shmairtsen*
travel sickness	die Reisekrankheit	*ryzer-krank-hite*
ulcer	das Geschwür	*gushvør*
vaccination	die Impfung	*impfoong*
to vomit	erbrechen	*airbreKHen*
whooping cough	der Keuchhusten	*koyKH-hOOsten*
wound	die Wunde	*voond-uh*

I have a pain in...
Ich habe Schmerzen in...
iKH ha-buh shmairtsen in

I do not feel well
Ich fühle mich nicht wohl
iKH føl-uh miKH niKHt vohl

I feel faint
Ich fühle mich schwach
iKH føl-uh miKH shvaKH

I feel sick
Ich fühle mich krank
iKH føl-uh miKH krank

I feel dizzy
Ich fühle mich schwindlig
iKH fOOl-uh miKH shvindliKH

It hurts here
Es tut hier weh
ess tOOt here vay

It's a sharp pain
Es ist ein heftiger Schmerz
ess ist ine heftiger shmairts

It's a dull pain
Es ist ein dumpfer Schmerz
ess ist ine doompfer shmairts

It hurts all the time
Es tut ständig weh
ess tOOt shtendiKH vay

It only hurts now and then
Es tut nur manchmal weh
ess tOOt nOOr manKHmahl vay

It hurts when you touch it
Es tut weh, wenn man daraufdrückt
ess tOOt vay ven man darowf-drOOkt

It hurts more at night
Nachts ist es schlimmer
naKHts ist ess shlimmer

It stings
Es brennt
ess brent

It aches
Es tut weh
ess tOOt vay

I need a prescription for...
Ich brauche ein Rezept für...
iKH browKH-uh ine retsept foor

I normally take...
Ich nehme normalerweise...
iKH name-uh normahler-vyz-uh

I'm allergic to...
Ich bin allergisch gegen...
iKH bin alairgish gaygen

Have you got anything for...?
Haben Sie etwas gegen...?
ha-ben zee etvas gaygen

Do I need a prescription for...?
Brauche ich ein Rezept für...?
browKH-uh iKH ine raytsept foor

I've lost a filling
Ich habe eine Plombe verloren
iKH hahb-uh ine-uh plomb-uh fairlor-en

REPLIES YOU MAY BE GIVEN

Nehmen Sie jeweils ... Tabletten
Take ... pills/tablets at a time

Mit Wasser/zum Zerkauen
With water/for chewing

Einmal/zweimal/dreimal täglich
Once/twice/three times a day

Nur vor dem Schlafengehen
Only when you go to bed

Morgens vor dem Frühstück
First thing in the morning

Was nehmen Sie sonst?
What do you normally take?

Sie sollten besser zum Arzt gehen
I think you should see a doctor

Tut mir leid, das haben wir nicht
I'm sorry, we don't have that

Dafür brauchen Sie ein Rezept
For that you need a prescription

Das ist hier nicht erhältlich
You can't get that here

THINGS YOU'LL SEE OR HEAR

Ambulanz	out-patients
Arzt	doctor
Augenarzt	optician
Augenoptiker	optician
Behandlung	treatment
Bereitschaftsdienst	duty chemist/doctor
der nächste bitte	next please!
Facharzt	specialist
Frauenarzt	gynaecologist
Hals, Nasen, Ohren	ear, nose and throat
Intensivstation	intensive care unit
Kinderarzt	paediatrician
Krankenhaus	hospital
Krankenkasse	health insurance
Krankenwagen	ambulance
Notfall	emergency
Orthopäde	orthopaedist
Privatpatient	private patient
Rezept	prescription
Sprechstunde	surgery
Termin	appointment
verschreiben	to prescribe
Wartezimmer	waiting room
Zahnarzt	dentist

CONVERSION TABLES

DISTANCES

Distances are marked in kilometres. To convert kilometres to miles divide the km. by 8 and multiply by 5 (one km. being five-eighths of a mile). Convert miles to km. by dividing the miles by 5 and multiplying by 8. A mile is 1609m. (1.609km.).

km.	miles *or* km.	miles
1.61	1	0.62
3.22	2	1.24
4.83	3	1.86
6.44	4	2.48
8.05	5	3.11
9.66	6	3.73
11.27	7	4.35
12.88	8	4.97
14.49	9	5.59
16.10	10	6.21
32.20	20	12.43
48.28	30	18.64
64.37	40	24.85
80.47	50	31.07
160.93	100	62.14
321.90	200	124.30
804.70	500	310.70
1609.34	1000	621.37

Other units of length:

1 centimetre	= 0.39 in.	1 inch	= 25.4 millimetres
1 metre	= 39.37 in.	1 foot	= 0.30 metre (30 cm.)
10 metres	= 32.81 ft.	1 yard	= 0.91 metre

WEIGHTS

The unit you will come into most contact with is the kilogram (kilo), equivalent to 2 lb 3 oz. To convert kg. to lbs., multiply by 2 and add one-tenth of the result (thus, 6 kg x 2 = 12 + 1.2, or 13.2 lbs). One ounce is about 28 grams, and 1 lb is 454 g. One UK hundredweight is almost 51 kg; one USA cwt is 45 kg. One UK ton is 1016 kg (USA ton = 907 kg).

grams	ounces	ounces	grams
50	1.76	1	28.3
100	3.53	2	56.7
250	8.81	4	113.4
500	17.63	8	226.8

kg.	lbs. or kg.	lbs.
0.45	1	2.20
0.91	2	4.41
1.36	3	6.61
1.81	4	8.82
2.27	5	11.02
2.72	6	13.23
3.17	7	15.43
3.63	8	17.64
4.08	9	19.84
4.53	10	22.04
9.07	20	44.09
11.34	25	55.11
22.68	50	110.23
45.36	100	220.46

CONVERSION TABLES

LIQUIDS

Motorists from the UK will be used to seeing petrol priced per litre (and may even know that one litre is about $1\frac{3}{4}$ pints). One 'imperial' gallon is roughly $4\frac{1}{2}$ litres, but USA drivers must remember that the American gallon is only 3.8 litres (1 litre = 1.06 US quart). In the following table, imperial gallons are used:

litres	gals. or l.	gals.
4.54	1	0.22
9.10	2	0.44
13.64	3	0.66
18.18	4	0.88
22.73	5	1.10
27.27	6	1.32
31.82	7	1.54
36.37	8	1.76
40.91	9	1.98
45.46	10	2.20
90.92	20	4.40
136.38	30	6.60
181.84	40	8.80
227.30	50	11.00

TYRE PRESSURES

lb/sq.in.	15	18	20	22	24
kg/sq.cm.	1.1	1.3	1.4	1.5	1.7

lb/sq.in.	26	28	30	33	35
kg/sq.cm.	1.8	2.0	2.1	2.3	2.5

AREA

The average tourist isn't all that likely to need metric area conversions, but with more 'holiday home' plots being bought overseas nowadays it might be useful to know that 1 square metre = 10.8 square feet, and that the main unit of land area measurement is a hectare (which is $2\frac{1}{2}$ acres). The hectare is 10,000 sq.m. - for convenience, visualise something roughly 100 metres or yards square. To convert hectares to acres, divide by 2 and multiply by 5 (and vice-versa).

hectares	acres or ha.	acres
0.4	**1**	2.5
2.0	**5**	12.4
4.1	**10**	24.7
20.2	**50**	123.6
40.5	**100**	247.1

TEMPERATURE

To convert centigrade or Celsius degrees into Fahrenheit, the accurate method is to multiply the °C figure by 1.8 and add 32. Similarly, to convert °F to °C, subtract 32 from the °F figure and divide by 1.8. This will give you a truly accurate conversion, but takes a little time in mental arithmetic! See the table below. If all you want is some idea of how hot it is forecast to be in the sun, simply double the °C figure and add 30; the °F result will be overstated by a degree or two when the answer is in the 60-80°F range, while 90°F should be 86°F.

°C	°F		°C	°F	
-10	14		25	77	
0	32		30	86	
5	41		36.9	98.4	body temperature
10	50		40	104	
20	68		100	212	boiling point

CLOTHING SIZES

Slight variations in sizes, let alone European equivalents of UK/USA sizes, will be found everywhere so be sure to check before you buy. The following tables are approximate:

Women's dresses and suits

UK	10	12	14	16	18	20
Europe	**36**	**38**	**40**	**42**	**44**	**46**
USA	8	10	12	14	16	18

Men's suits and coats

UK/USA	36	38	40	42	44	46
Europe	**46**	**48**	**50**	**52**	**54**	**56**

Women's shoes

UK	4	5	6	7	8
Europe	**37**	**38**	**39**	**41**	**42**
USA	$5\frac{1}{2}$	$6\frac{1}{2}$	$7\frac{1}{2}$	$8\frac{1}{2}$	$9\frac{1}{2}$

Men's shoes

UK/USA	7	8	9	10	11
Europe	**41**	**42**	**43**	**44**	**45**

Men's shirts

UK/USA	14	$14\frac{1}{2}$	15	$15\frac{1}{2}$	16	$16\frac{1}{2}$	17
Europe	**36**	**37**	**38**	**39**	**41**	**42**	**43**

Women's sweaters

UK/USA	32	34	36	38	40
Europe	**36**	**38**	**40**	**42**	**44**

Waist and chest measurements

Inches	28	30	32	34	36	38	40	42	44	46
Cms	71	76	80	87	91	97	102	107	112	117

(adj) chinesisch
chips die Pommes frites
chocolate die Schokolade
  box of chocolates die
  Pralinenschachtel
  bar of chocolate die Tafel
  Schokolade
chop *(food)* das Kotelett
  (to cut) kleinschneiden
church die Kirche
cigar die Zigarre
cigarette die Zigarette
cinema das Kino
city die (Groß)stadt
city centre das Stadtzentrum
class die Klasse
classical music die klassische
  Musik
clean sauber
clear klar
  is that clear? ist das klar?
clever klug
clock die Uhr
  (alarm) der Wecker
close *(near)* nah
  (stuffy) stickig
close *(verb)* schließen
  the shop is closed der Laden
  ist geschlossen
clothes die Kleider
club *(society)* der Verein
  (golf etc) der Klub
  (cards) Kreuz
clutch die Kupplung
coach der Bus
  (of train) der Waggon
coach station der Busbahnhof
coat der Mantel
coathanger der (Kleider)bügel
cockroach die Küchenschabe
coffee der Kaffee
coin die Münze

cold *(illness)* die Erkältung
  (adj) kalt
collar der Kragen
collection *(stamps etc)* die
  Sammlung
  (postal) die Leerung
colour die Farbe
colour film der Farbfilm
comb *(noun)* der Kamm
  (verb) kämmen
come kommen
  I come from ... ich komme
  aus ...
  we came last week wir sind
  letzte Woche angekommen
communication cord die
  Notbremse
compact disc die Compact-Disc
compartment das Abteil
complicated kompliziert
concert das Konzert
conditioner *(hair)* der Festiger
conductor *(bus)* der Schaffner
  (orchestra) der Dirigent
congratulations! herzlichen
  Glückwunsch!
constipation die Verstopfung
consulate das Konsulat
contact lenses die Kontaktlinsen
contraceptive das
  Verhütungsmittel
cook *(noun)* der Koch
  (verb) kochen
cooking utensils das
  Kochgeschirr
cool kühl
cork der Korken
corkscrew der Korkenzieher
corner die Ecke
corridor der Korridor
  (in train) der Gang
cosmetics Kosmetika

cost *(verb)* kosten
  what does it cost? was kostet das?
cotton die Baumwolle
cotton wool die Watte
cough *(verb)* husten
  (noun) der Husten
council der Rat
country *(state)* das Land
  (not town) das Land
cousin *(male)* der Vetter, der Cousin
  (female) die Kusine
crab die Krabbe
cramp der Krampf
crayfish der Krebs
cream *(for cake etc)* die Sahne
  (lotion) die Creme
credit card die Kreditkarte
crew die Mannschaft
  (plane etc) die Besatzung
crisps die Chips
crowded überfüllt
cruise die Kreuzfahrt
crutches die Krücken
cry *(weep)* weinen
  (shout) rufen
cucumber die Gurke
cufflinks die Manschettenknöpfe
cup die Tasse
cupboard der Schrank
curlers die Lockenwickler
curls die Locken
curry der Curry
curtain der Vorhang
cut *(noun)* der Schnitt
  (verb) schneiden

dad der Vati
dairy *(shop)* das Milchgeschäft

Dane der Däne/die Dänin
Danish dänisch
dark dunkel
daughter die Tochter
day der Tag
dead tot
deaf taub
dear *(expensive)* teuer
  (cherished) lieb
deckchair der Liegestuhl
deep tief
deliberately absichtlich
Denmark Dänemark
dentist der Zahnarzt
dentures die Prothese
deny bestreiten
deodorant das Deodorant
department store das Kaufhaus
departure die Abfahrt
develop *(grow)* sich entwickeln
  (a film) entwickeln
diamond *(jewel)* der Diamant
  (cards) Karo
diarrhoea der Durchfall
diary das Tagebuch
dictionary das Wörterbuch
die sterben
diesel der Diesel
different verschieden
  that's different das ist etwas anderes
  I'd like a different kind ich möchte gern eine andere Sorte
difficult schwierig
dining car der Speisewagen
dining room der Speiseraum
directory das Verzeichnis
  (telephone) das Telefonbuch
dirty schmutzig
disabled *(person)* der/die Behinderte
  (adj) behindert

distributor *(car)* der Verteiler
dive tauchen
diving board das Sprungbrett
divorced geschieden
do tun
doctor der Arzt
document die Urkunde
dog der Hund
doll die Puppe
dollar der Dollar
door die Tür
double room das Doppelzimmer
doughnut der Berliner
down herunter
  (position) unten
drawing pin die Heftzwecke
dress das Kleid
drink *(verb)* trinken
  (noun) das Getränk
  would you like a drink?
  möchten Sie etwas trinken?
drinking water das Trinkwasser
drive *(verb: car)* fahren
driver der Fahrer
driving licence der Führerschein
drunk betrunken
dry trocken
dry cleaner die chemische
  Reinigung
during während
dustbin die Mülltonne
duster das Staubtuch
Dutch holländisch
Dutchman der Holländer
duty-free zollfrei

each *(every)* jede(r/s)
  two marks each zwei Mark
  das Stück
early früh

earrings die Ohrringe
ears die Ohren
east der Osten
East Germany die DDR
easy leicht
egg das Ei
egg cup der Eierbecher
either: either of them eine(r)
  von beiden
  either... or entweder... oder
elastic elastisch
elastic band das Gummiband
elbows die Ellenbogen
electric elektrisch
electricity der Strom
else: something else etwas
  anderes
  someone else ein anderer
  somewhere else woanders
embarrassing peinlich
embassy die Botschaft
embroidery die Stickerei
emerald der Smaragd
emergency der Notfall
empty leer
end das Ende
engaged *(couple)* verlobt
  (occupied) besetzt
engine *(motor)* der Motor
  (railway) die Lokomotive
England England
English *(adj)* englisch
Englishman der Engländer
Englishwoman die Engländerin
enlargement die Vergrößerung
enough genug
entertainment die Unterhaltung
entrance der Eingang
envelope der (Brief)umschlag
escalator die Rolltreppe
especially besonders
evening der Abend

111

every jede(r/s)
everyone jeder
everything alles
everywhere überall
example das Beispiel
   for example zum Beispiel
excellent ausgezeichnet
excess baggage das Übergewicht
exchange *(verb)* (um)tauschen
exchange rate der Wechselkurs
excursion der Ausflug
exit *(noun)* der Ausgang
expensive teuer
extension lead die
   Verlängerungsschnur
eye drops die Augentropfen
eyes die Augen

face das Gesicht
faint *(unclear)* blaß
   (verb) ohnmächtig werden
   to feel faint sich schwach
   fühlen
fair *(funfair)* der Jahrmarkt
   (just) gerecht, fair
   it's not fair das ist ungerecht
false teeth die Prothese
fan *(ventilator)* der Ventilator
   (enthusiast) der Fan
fan belt der Keilriemen
far weit
fare der Fahrpreis
farm der Bauernhof
farmer der Bauer
fashion die Mode
fast schnell
fat *(of person)* dick
   (on meat etc) das Fett
father der Vater
feel *(touch)* fühlen

I feel hot mir ist heiß
I feel like... Ich möchte gern...
I don't feel well mir ist nicht
gut
feet die Füße
felt-tip pen der Filzstift
ferry die Fähre
fever das Fieber
fiancé der Verlobte
fiancée die Verlobte
field das Feld
fig die Feige
filling *(tooth)* die Füllung
   (sandwich etc) der Belag
film der Film
finger der Finger
fire das Feuer
fire extinguisher der
   Feuerlöscher
firework das Feuerwerk
first erste(r/s)
first aid die Erste Hilfe
first floor der erste Stock
fish der Fisch
fishing das Angeln
   to go fishing Angeln gehen
fishing rod die Angelrute
fishmonger der Fischhändler
fizzy sprudelnd
flag die Fahne
flash *(camera)* der Blitz
flat *(level)* flach
   (apartment) die Wohnung
flavour der Geschmack
flight der Flug
flip-flops die Gummilatschen
flippers die (Schwimm)flossen
flour das Mehl
flower die Blume
flu die Grippe
flute die Flöte
fly *(verb)* fliegen

(insect) die Fliege
fog der Nebel
folk music die Volksmusik
food das Essen
food poisoning die Lebensmittelvergiftung
foot der Fuß
football der Fußball
for für
  for me für mich
  what for? wofür?
  for a week für eine Woche
foreigner der Ausländer/die Ausländerin
forest der Wald
fork die Gabel
fortnight zwei Wochen
fountain pen der Füller
fracture der Bruch
France Frankreich
free *(no cost)* kostenlos
  (at liberty) frei
freezer der Gefrierschrank
French französisch
Frenchman der Franzose
Frenchwoman die Französin
fridge der Kühlschrank
friend der Freund/die Freundin
friendly freundlich
from von
front: in front vorn
frost der Frost
fruit die Frucht
fruit juice der Fruchtsaft
fry braten
frying pan die (Brat)pfanne
full voll
  I'm full ich binn satt
full board Vollpension
funnel *(for pouring)* der Trichter
funny komisch
furniture die Möbel

garage *(to park car)* die Garage
  (for repairs) die Werkstatt
garden der Garten
garlic der Knoblauch
gas-permeable lenses luftdurchlässige Kontaktlinsen
gay *(happy)* fröhlich
  (homosexual) schwul
gear der Gang
gear lever der Schaltknüppel
gents *(toilet)* die Herrentoilette
German *(person)* der/die Deutsche
  (adj) deutsch
Germany Deutschland
get *(fetch)* holen
  have you got ...? haben Sie ...?
  to get the train den Zug nehmen
get back: we get back tomorrow wir kommen morgen zurück
  to get something back etwas zurückbekommen
get in hereinkommen
  (arrive) ankommen
get out herauskommen
  (bring out) herausholen
get up *(rise)* aufstehen
gift das Geschenk
gin der Gin
ginger der Ingwer
girl das Mädchen
girlfriend die Freundin
give geben
glad froh
  I'm glad ich bin froh
glass das Glas
glasses die Brille
gloss prints die Glanzabzüge

113

gloves die Handschuhe
glue der Leim
goggles die Schutzbrille
gold das Gold
good gut
goodbye auf Wiedersehen
government die Regierung
grapes die Trauben
grass das Gras
green grün
grey grau
grill der Grill
grocer *(shop)* das
  Lebensmittelgeschäft
ground floor das Erdgeschoß
ground sheet die Bodenplane
guarantee *(noun)* die Garantie
  (verb) garantieren
guard der Wächter
  (train) der Schaffner
guide book der (Reise)führer
guitar die Gitarre
gun *(rifle)* das Gewehr
  (pistol) die Pistole

hair das Haar
haircut der Haarschnitt
hairdresser der Friseur
hair dryer der Haartrockner
hair spray das Haarspray
half halb
  half an hour eine halbe Stunde
half board Halbpension
ham der Schinken
hamburger der Hamburger
hammer der Hammer
hand die Hand
hand brake die Handbremse
handbag die Handtasche
handkerchief das Taschentuch

handle *(door)* die Klinke
handsome gutaussehend
hangover der Kater
happy glücklich
harbour der Hafen
hard hart
  (difficult) schwer
hard lenses harte Kontaktlinsen
hat der Hut
have haben
  can I have...? kann ich ...
  bekommen?
  have you got...? haben Sie...?
  I have to go now ich muß jetzt
  gehen
hayfever der Heuschnupfen
he er
head der Kopf
headache die Kopfschmerzen
headlights die Scheinwerfer
hear hören
hearing aid das Hörgerät
heart das Herz
  (cards) Herz
heart attack der Herzinfarkt
heating die Heizung
heavy schwer
heel *(shoe)* der Absatz
  (foot) die Ferse
hello guten Tag
  (to get attention) hallo
help *(noun)* die Hilfe
  (verb) helfen
  help! Hilfe!
her: it's her sie ist es
  it's hers es gehört ihr
  it's for her es ist für sie
  give it to her geben Sie es ihr
hi hallo
high hoch
highway code die
  Straßenverkehrsordnung

hill der Berg
him: it's him er ist es
  it's for him es ist für ihn
  give it to him geben Sie es ihm
his sein
  it's his es gehört ihm
history die Geschichte
hitch hike trampen
hobby das Hobby
holiday der Urlaub
Holland Holland
honest ehrlich
honey der Honig
honeymoon die Flitterwochen
horn *(car)* die Hupe
  (animal) das Horn
horrible schrecklich
hospital das Krankenhaus
hot water bottle die Wärmflasche
hour die Stunde
house das Haus
how? wie?
hungry hungrig
  I'm hungry ich habe Hunger
husband der (Ehe)mann

I ich
ice das Eis
ice cream das Eis, die Eiskrem
ice cube der Eiswürfel
ice lolly das Eis am Stiel
ice rink die Eisbahn
ice-skates die Schlittschuhe
if wenn
India Indien
Indian *(person)* der Inder/
  die Inderin
  (adj) indisch
ignition die Zündung
immediately sofort

impossible unmöglich
in in
indicator der Blinker
indigestion die
  Magenverstimmung
infection die Infektion
information die Information
injection die Spritze
injury die Verletzung
ink die Tinte
inn das Gasthaus
inner tube der Schlauch
insect das Insekt
insect repellent das
  Insektenmittel
insomnia die Schlaflosigkeit
insurance die Versicherung
interesting interessant
invitation die Einladung
Ireland Irland
Irish *(adj)* irisch
Irishman der Ire
Irishwoman die Irin
iron *(metal)* das Eisen
  (for clothes) das Bügeleisen
ironmonger die
  Eisenwarenhandlung
is: he/she/it is er/sie/es ist
island die Insel
it es
Italian *(person)* der Italiener/die
  Italienerin
  (adj) italienisch
Italy Italien
itch *(noun)* das Jucken
  (verb) jucken
  it itches es juckt

jacket die Jacke
jacuzzi der Whirlpool

jam die Marmelade
jazz der Jazz
jealous eifersüchtig
jeans die Jeans
jellyfish die Qualle
jeweller der Juwelier
job die Arbeit
jog *(verb)* joggen
  to go for a jog joggen gehen
joke der Witz
journey die Reise
jumper der Pullover
just: it's just arrived es ist
  gerade angekommen
  I've just one left ich habe nur
  noch eine(n/s)

kettle der Wasserkessel
key der Schlüssel
kidney die Niere
kilo das Kilo
kilometre der Kilometer
kitchen die Küche
knee das Knie
knife das Messer
knit stricken
knitting needle die Stricknadel

label das Etikett
lace die Spitze
  (of shoe) der Schnürsenkel
ladies *(toilet)* die Damentoilette
lake der See
lamb das Lamm
lamp die Lampe
lampshade der Lampenschirm
land *(noun)* das Land
  (verb) landen

language die Sprache
large groß
last *(final)* letzte(r,s)
  last week/month letzte Woche/
  letzten Monat
  at last endlich!
late: it's getting late es wird
  spät
  the bus is late der Bus hat
  Verspätung
laugh lachen
launderette der Waschsalon
laundry *(place)* die Wäscherei
  (clothes) die Wäsche
laxative das Abführmittel
lazy faul
leaf das Blatt
learn lernen
leather das Leder
left *(not right)* links
  (remaining) übrig
  there's nothing left es ist
  nichts mehr übrig
left luggage die Gepäck-
  aufbewahrung
  (locker) das Gepäckschließfach
leftovers die Überreste
leg das Bein
lemon die Zitrone
lemonade die Limonade
length die Länge
lens die Linse
less weniger
lesson die Stunde
letter *(post)* der Brief
  (alphabet) der Buchstabe
letterbox der Briefkasten
lettuce der Kopfsalat
library die Bücherei
licence die Genehmigung
Liechtenstein Liechtenstein
life das Leben

lift *(in building)* der Fahrstuhl
  (in car) die Mitfahrgelegenheit
  to give someone a lift
  jemanden mitnehmen
light *(not heavy)* leicht
  (not dark) hell
light meter der Belichtungsmesser
lighter das Feuerzeug
lighter fuel das Feuerzeugbenzin
like: I like you Ich mag Sie
  I like swimming ich schwimme
  gern
  it's like ... es ist wie ...
lime *(fruit)* die Limone
lip salve der Lippen-Fettstift
lipstick der Lippenstift
liqueur der Likör
list die Liste
litre der Liter
litter der Abfall
little *(small)* klein
  it's a little big es ist ein
  bißchen zu groß
liver die Leber
lobster der Hummer
lollipop der Lutscher
lorry der Lastwagen
lost property office das
  Fundbüro
lot: a lot viel
loud laut
  (colour) grell
lounge *(in house)* das Wohnzimmer
  (in hotel etc) der Salon
love: *(noun)* die Liebe
  I love you ich liebe dich
low niedrig
  (voice) leise
luck das Glück
  good luck! viel Glück!
luggage das Gepäck
luggage rack die Gepäckablage

lunch das Mittagessen
Luxembourg Luxemburg

magazine die Zeitschrift
mail die Post
make machen
man der Mann
manager der Geschäftsführer
map die Landkarte
  (street map) der Straßenplan
margarine die Margarine
market der Markt
marmalade die
  Orangenmarmelade
married verheiratet
mascara die Wimperntusche
mass *(church)* die Messe
match *(light)* das Streichholz
  (sport) das Spiel
material *(cloth)* der Stoff
mattress die Matratze
maybe vielleicht
me: it's me ich bin's
  it's for me es ist für mich
  give it to me gib es mir
meal das Essen
meat das Fleisch
mechanic der Mechaniker
medicine die Medizin
Mediterranean *(noun)* das
  Mittelmeer
meeting das Treffen
melon die Melone
menu die Speisekarte
message die Nachricht
midday der Mittag
middle die Mitte
midnight Mitternacht
milk die Milch
mine: it's mine es gehört mir
mineral water das Mineralwasser

mirror der Spiegel
mistake der Fehler
  to make a mistake einen
  Fehler machen
money das Geld
month der Monat
monument das Denkmal
moped das Moped
more mehr
  more or less mehr oder weniger
morning der Morgen
  in the morning am Morgen
mother die Mutter
motorbike das Motorrad
motorboat das Motorboot
motorway die Autobahn
mountain der Berg
moustache der Schnurrbart
mouth der Mund
move *(verb)* bewegen
  I can't move ich kann mich
  nicht bewegen
  to move house umziehen
much: not much nicht viel
mug die Tasse
mum die Mutti
museum das Museum
mushroom der Pilz
music die Musik
musical instrument das
  Musikinstrument
musician der Musiker
mussels die Muscheln
mustard der Senf
my mein(e)
  that's my book das ist mein
  Buch

nail *(metal, finger)* der Nagel
nail file die Nagelfeile

nail polish der Nagellack
narrow eng
near nah
  near the door nahe der Tür
  near London in der Nähe von
  London
neck der Hals
necklace die Halskette
need *(verb)* brauchen;
  I need ... ich brauche
  there's no need to... es ist
  nicht nötig, zu...
needle die Nadel
negative *(photo)* das Negativ
  (no) negativ
neither: neither of them keiner
  von Ihnen
  neither ... nor weder ... noch
nephew der Neffe
never nie
new neu
news die Nachrichten
newsagent der Zeitungshändler
newspaper die Zeitung
New Zealand Neuseeland
next nächste(r/s);
  next week/month nächste
  Woche/nächsten Monat
  what next? sonst noch was?
niece die Nichte
night die Nacht
nightclub der Nachtklub
nightdress das Nachthemd
no *(response)* nein
  (not any) kein(e)
noisy laut
north der Norden
Norway Norwegen
Norwegian *(person)* der Norweger/
  die Norwegerin
  (adj) norwegisch
nose die Nase

nose drops die Nasentropfen
not nicht
notebook das Notizbuch
novel der Roman
now jetzt
nudist der Nudist/die Nudistin
number die Zahl
  (telephone) die Nummer
number plate das
  Nummernschild
nurse die Krankenschwester
nursery slope der Idiotenhügel
nut *(fruit)* die Nuß
  (for bolt) die Mutter

occasionally gelegentlich
office das Büro
often oft
oil das Öl
ointment die Salbe
old alt
olive die Olive
omelette das Omelette
on auf
onion die Zwiebel
open *(verb)* öffnen
  (adj) offen
operator *(phone)* die Vermittlung
opposite *(adj)* gegenüber
optician der Augenarzt
or oder
orange *(colour)* orange
  (fruit) die Orange
orchestra das Orchester
organ das Organ
  (music) die Orgel
our unser
  it's ours es gehört uns
out: he's out er ist nicht da
outside außerhalb

over über
  over there dort drüben
overtake überholen
oyster die Auster

pack of cards das Kartenspiel
package die Schachtel
  (parcel) das Paket
packet das Paket
  (small box) die Schachtel
  a packet of ... eine Schachtel...
page die Seite
pain der Schmerz
pair das Paar
Pakistan Pakistan
Pakistani *(person)* der Pakistani/
  die Pakistanerin
  (adj) pakistanisch
pancake der Pfannkuchen
paracetamol die
  Kopfschmerztablette
paraffin das Paraffin
parcel das Paket
pardon? bitte?
parents die Eltern
park *(noun)* der Park
  (verb) parken
parsley die Petersilie
party *(celebration)* die Party
  (group) die Gesellschaft
  (political) die Partei
passenger der Passagier
passport der Paß
pasta die Nudeln
path der Weg
pay bezahlen
peach der Pfirsich
peanuts die Erdnüsse
pear die Birne
pearl die Perle

peas die Erbsen
pedestrian der Fußgänger/ die Fußgängerin
peg *(clothes)* der Aufhänger
pen der Stift
pencil der Bleistift
pencil sharpener der Bleistiftspitzer
penfriend der Brieffreund/ die Brieffreundin
penknife das Taschenmesser
pepper *(& salt)* der Pfeffer *(red/green)* der Paprika
peppermints die Pfefferminzbonbons
perfume das Parfüm
perhaps vielleicht
perm die Dauerwelle
petrol das Benzin
petrol station die Tankstelle
petticoat der Unterrock
photograph *(noun)* das Bild *(verb)* fotografieren
photographer der Fotograf
phrase book der Sprachführer
piano das Klavier
pickpocket der Taschendieb
picnic das Picknick
piece das Stück
pillow das Kopfkissen
pilot der Pilot
pin die Stecknadel
pineapple die Ananas
pink rosa
pipe *(for smoking)* die Pfeife *(for water)* das Rohr
piston der Kolben
piston ring der Kolbenring
pizza die Pizza
plant die Pflanze
plaster *(for cut)* das Pflaster
plastic das Plastik

plastic bag die Plastiktüte
plate der Teller
platform der Bahnsteig
please bitte
plug *(electrical)* der Stecker *(sink)* der Stopfen
pocket die Tasche
poison das Gift
police station das Polizeirevier
policeman der Polizist
politics die Politik
poor arm *(bad quality)* schlecht
pop music die Popmusik
pork das Schweinefleisch
port *(harbour)* der Hafen *(drink)* der Portwein
porter der Portier
Portugal Portugal
Portuguese *(person)* der Portugiese/die Portugiesin *(adj)* portugiesisch
post *(noun)* die Post *(verb)* aufgeben
post box der Briefkasten
postcard die Postkarte
poster das Poster
postman der Briefträger
post office das Postamt
potato die Kartoffel
pound *(weight, money)* das Pfund
poultry das Geflügel
powder das Pulver *(cosmetics)* der Puder
pram der Kinderwagen
prawn die Krabbe
prescription das Rezept
pretty *(beautiful)* schön *(quite)* ziemlich
priest der Geistliche
private privat
problem das Problem

what's the problem? wo fehlt's?
public öffentlich
pull ziehen
purple lila
purse das Portemonnaie
push drücken
pushchair der Sportwagen
pyjamas der Schlafanzug

quality die Qualität
quay der Kai
question die Frage
queue *(noun)* die Schlange
(verb) Schlange stehen
quick schnell
quiet ruhig
quilt das Federbett
quite ganz

radiator *(heating)* der Heizkörper
(car) der Kühler
radio das Radio
radish der Rettich
(small red) das Radieschen
railway line die Bahngleise
rain der Regen
raincoat der Regenmantel
raisin die Rosine
rare *(uncommon)* selten
(steak) englisch
raspberry die Himbeere
razor blades die Rasierklingen
reading lamp die Leselampe
ready fertig
rear lights die Rücklichter
receipt die Quittung
receptionist die Empfangsperson

record *(music)* die Schallplatte
(sporting etc) der Rekord
record player der Plattenspieler
record shop das Schallplatten-geschäft
red rot
refreshments die Erfrischungen
registered letter der Einschreibebrief
relax sich entspannen
religion die Religion
remember sich erinnern
reservation die Reservierung
rest *(remainder)* der Rest
(relax) sich ausruhen
restaurant das Restaurant
restaurant car der Speisewagen
return *(come back)* zurück-kommen
(give back) zurückgeben
rice der Reis
rich reich
right *(correct)* richtig
(direction) rechts
ring *(to call)* anrufen
(wedding etc) der Ring
ripe reif
river der Fluß
road die Straße
rock *(stone)* der Stein
(music) der Rock
roll *(bread)* das Brötchen
(verb) rollen
roller skates die Rollschuhe
room das Zimmer
(space) der Raum
rope das Seil
rose die Rose
round *(circular)* rund
it's my round das ist meine Runde
rowing boat das Ruderboot

rubber *(eraser)* der Radiergummi
  (material) das Gummi
rubbish der Abfall
ruby *(colour)* rubinrot
  (stone) der Rubin
rucksack der Rucksack
rug *(mat)* der Läufer
  (blanket) die Wolldecke
ruins die Ruinen
ruler das Lineal
rum der Rum
runway die Start- und Landebahn

sad traurig
safe sicher
safety pin die Sicherheitsnadel
sailing boat das Segelboot
salad der Salat
salami die Salami
sale der Verkauf
  (at reduced prices) der
  Schlußverkauf
salmon der Lachs
salt das Salz
same: the same der/die/dasselbe
sand der Sand
sandals die Sandalen
sand dunes die Sanddünen
sandwich das Butterbrot
sanitary towels die Damenbinden
sauce die Soße
saucepan der Kochtopf
sauna die Sauna
sausage die Wurst
say sagen
  what did you say? was haben
  Sie gesagt?
  how do you say ...? wie sagt
  man ...?
scampi die Scampi

Scandanavia Skandinavien
Scandinavian *(person)* der
  Skandinavier/die Skandinavierin
  (adj) skandinavisch
scarf der Schal
school die Schule
scissors die Schere
Scot der Schotte/die Schottin
Scotland Schottland
Scottish schottisch
screw die Schraube
screwdriver der Schraubenzieher
sea das Meer
seat der Sitz
seat belt der Sicherheitsgurt
see sehen
  I can't see ich kann nichts
  sehen
  I see! ich verstehe!
sell verkaufen
sellotape (R) der Tesafilm (R)
serious ernst
serviette die Serviette
several mehrere
sew nähen
shampoo das Shampoo
shave *(noun)* die Rasur
  (verb) sich rasieren
shaving foam die Rasiercreme
shawl das Umhängetuch
she sie
sheet das (Bett)laken
shell die Muschel
sherry der Sherry
ship das Schiff
shirt das Hemd
shoe laces die Schnürsenkel
shoe polish die Schuhcreme
shoe shop das Schuhgeschäft
shoes die Schuhe
shop das Geschäft
shopping: to go shopping

einkaufen gehen
shopping centre das
Einkaufszentrum
short kurz
shorts die Shorts
shoulder die Schulter
shower *(bath)* die Dusche
(rain) der Schauer
shrimp die Garnele
shutter *(camera)* der Verschluß
(window) der Fensterladen
sick *(ill)* krank
I feel sick mir ist übel
side die Seite
(edge) die Kante
I'm on his side ich stehe auf
seiner Seite
sidelights das Standlicht
silk die Seide
silver *(colour)* silber
(metal) das Silber
simple einfach
sing singen
single *(one)* einzige(r/s)
(unmarried) unverheiratet
single room das Einzelzimmer
sister die Schwester
skates die Schlittschuhe
ski *(noun)* der Ski
(verb) Ski fahren
to go skiing Ski fahren gehen
skid *(verb)* schleudern
ski-lift der Skilift
skin cleanser der Hautreiniger
skirt der Rock
sky der Himmel
ski stick der Skistock
sledge der Schlitten
sleep *(noun)* der Schlaf
(verb) schlafen
to go to sleep schlafen gehen
sleeping bag der Schlafsack

sleeping car der Schlafwagen
sleeping pill die Schlaftablette
sling die Schlinge
slippers die Pantoffeln
slow langsam
small klein
smell *(noun)* der Geruch
(verb) riechen
smile *(noun)* das Lächeln
(verb) lächeln
smoke *(noun)* der Rauch
(verb) rauchen
snack der Imbiß
snorkel der Schnorchel
snow der Schnee
so so
soaking solution *(for contact
lenses)* die Aufbewahrungslösung
soap die Seife
socks die Strümpfe
soda water das Sodawasser
soft lenses weiche Kontaktlinsen
somebody (irgend)jemand
somehow irgendwie
something etwas
sometimes manchmal
somewhere irgendwo
son der Sohn
song das Lied
sorry: I'm sorry es tut mir leid
soup die Suppe
south der Süden
South Africa Südafrika
souvenir das Souvenir
spade *(shovel)* der Spaten
(cards) Pik
Spain Spanien
Spaniard der Spanier
Spanish spanisch
she's Spanish sie ist Spanierin
spanner der Schraubenschlüssel
spares die Ersatzteile

123

spark(ing) plug die Zündkerze
speak sprechen
  I don't speak German ich
  spreche kein Deutsch
speed die Geschwindigkeit
speed limit die Geschwindigkeits-
  beschränkung
speedometer der Tacho(meter)
spider die Spinne
spinach der Spinat
spoon der Löffel
sprain die Verstauchung
spring *(mechanical)* die Feder
  (season) der Frühling
stadium das Stadion
staircase die Treppe
stairs die Treppe
stamp die Briefmarke
stapler der Hefter
star der Stern
  (film) der Star
start *(noun)* der Start, der Anfang
  (verb) anfangen
station der Bahnhof
  (tube) die U-Bahn-Station
statue die Statue
steak das Steak
steamer der Dampfer
steering wheel das Lenkrad
steward der Steward
sting *(noun)* der Stich
  (verb) stechen
  it stings es brennt
stockings die Strümpfe
stomach der Magen
stomach-ache die
  Magenschmerzen
stop *(verb)* anhalten
  (bus stop) die Haltestelle
  stop! halt!
storm der Sturm
strawberry die Erdbeere

stream *(small river)* der Bach
string *(cord)* der Faden
  (guitar etc) die Saite
student der Student
stupid dumm
suburbs der Stadtrand
sugar der Zucker
suit *(noun)* der Anzug
  (verb) passen
  it suits you es steht Ihnen
suitcase der Koffer
sun die Sonne
sunbathe sonnenbaden
sunburn der Sonnenbrand
sunglasses die Sonnenbrille
sunny sonnig
suntan die Sonnenbräune
suntan lotion das Sonnenöl
supermarket der Supermarkt
supplement der Zuschlag
sweat *(verb)* schwitzen
  (noun) der Schweiß
sweatshirt das Sweatshirt
Swede der Schwede/die Schwedin
Sweden Schweden
Swedish schwedisch
sweet *(not sour)* süß
  (candy) die Süßigkeit
swimming costume das
  Badekostüm
swimming pool das Schwimmbad
swimming trunks die Badehose
Swiss *(person)* der Schweizer/die
  Schweizerin
  (adj) schweizerisch
switch der Schalter
Switzerland die Schweiz

table der Tisch
tablet die Tablette

take nehmen
take-away *(shop)* die Imbißstube
  (meal) der Imbiß
take off *(plane)* der Abflug
  (verb) abfliegen
talcum powder das Körperpuder
talk *(verb)* reden
  (noun) das Gespräch
tall groß
tampon das Tampon
tangerine die Mandarine
tap der Hahn
tapestry der Wandteppich
tea der Tee
tea towel das Geschirrtuch
telegram das Telegramm
telephone *(noun)* das Telefon
  (verb) telefonieren
telephone box die Telefonzelle
telephone call das
  Telefongespräch
television das Fernsehen
temperature *(heat)* die
  Temperatur
  (fever) das Fieber
tent das Zelt
tent peg der Hering
tent pole die Zeltstange
than: bigger than größer als
thank *(verb)* danken
  thanks danke
  thank you vielen Dank
that: that man dieser Mann
  that woman diese Frau
  what's that? was ist das?
  I think that... ich denke, daß...
their ihr
  it's theirs es gehört ihnen
them: it's them sie sind es
  it's for them es ist für sie
  give it to them geben Sie es
  ihnen

then dann
there da
thermos flask die Thermosflasche
these: these things diese Dinge
  these are mine diese gehören
  mir
they sie
thick dick
thin dünn
think denken
  I think so ich glaube schon
  I'll think about it ich werde
  darüber nachdenken
thirsty durstig
  I'm thirsty Ich habe Durst
this: this man dieser Mann
  this woman diese Frau
  what's this? was ist das?
those: those things die Dinge
  dort
  those are his diese da gehören
  ihm
throat die Kehle
throat pastilles Halstabletten
through durch
thunderstorm das Gewitter
ticket die Fahrkarte
tie *(noun)* die Krawatte
  (verb) festmachen
tight eng
tights die Strumpfhose
time die Zeit
  what's the time? wie spät ist
  es?
timetable der Fahrplan
tin die Dose
tin opener der Dosenöffner
tip *(money)* das Trinkgeld
  (end) die Spitze
tired müde
  I feel tired ich bin müde
tissues Papiertücher

to: to England nach England
to the station zum Bahnhof
to the bus stop zur
Bushaltestelle
toast der Toast
tobacco der Tabak
toboggan der Schlitten
today heute
together zusammen
toilet die Toilette
toilet paper das Toilettenpapier
tomato die Tomate
tomorrow morgen
tongue die Zunge
tonic das Tonic(wasser)
tonight heute abend
too *(also)* auch
(excessive) zu
tooth der Zahn
toothache Zahnschmerzen
toothbrush die Zahnbürste
toothpaste die Zahnpasta
torch die Taschenlampe
tour die Rundreise
tourist der Tourist
towel das Handtuch
tower der Turm
town die Stadt
town hall das Rathaus
toy das Spielzeug
toy shop der Spielzeugladen
track suit der Trainingsanzug
tractor der Traktor
tradition die Tradition
traffic der Verkehr
traffic lights die Ampel
trailer der Anhänger
train der Zug
translate übersetzen
transmission die Übertragung
travel agency das Reisebüro
traveller's cheque der

Reisescheck
tray das Tablett
tree der Baum
trousers die Hose
try versuchen
tunnel der Tunnel
tweezers die Pinzette
typewriter die Schreibmaschine
tyre der Reifen

umbrella der (Regen)schirm
uncle der Onkel
under unter
underground die U-Bahn
underpants die Unterhose
university die Universität
unmarried unverheiratet
until bis
unusual ungewöhnlich
up oben
(upwards) nach oben
urgent dringend
us: it's us wir sind es
it's for us es ist für uns
give it to us geben Sie es uns
use *(noun)* der Gebrauch
(verb) gebrauchen
it's no use es hat keinen Zweck
useful hilfreich
usual gewöhnlich
usually gewöhnlich

vacancy eine freie Stelle
(room) ein freies Zimmer
vacuum cleaner der Staubsauger
vacuum flask die Thermosflasche
valley das Tal
valve das Ventil

vanilla die Vanille
vase die Vase
veal das Kalbfleisch
vegetables des Gemüse
vegetarian *(person)* der Vegetarier/
  die Vegetarierin
  (adj) vegetarisch
vehicle das Fahrzeug
very sehr
vest das Unterhemd
view der Blick
viewfinder der Sucher
villa die Villa
village das Dorf
vinegar der Essig
violin die Violine
visa das Visum
visit *(noun)* der Besuch
  (verb) besuchen
visitor der Besucher/die
  Besucherin
vitamin tablet die Vitamintablette
vodka der Wodka
voice die Stimme

wait warten
waiter der Ober
  waiter! Herr Ober!
waiting room das Wartezimmer
  (station) der Wartesaal
waitress die Kellnerin
Wales Wales
walk *(verb)* gehen
  (noun) der Spaziergang
  to go for a walk spazieren
  gehen
walkman (R) der Walkman (R)
wall *(inside)* die Wand
  (outside) die Mauer
wallet die Brieftasche

war der Krieg
wardrobe der Kleiderschrank
warm warm
was: I was ich war
  he/she/it was er/sie/es war
washing powder das Waschpulver
washing-up liquid das Spülmittel
wasp die Wespe
watch *(noun)* die (Armband)uhr
  (verb) ansehen
water das Wasser
waterfall der Wasserfall
wave *(noun)* die Welle
  (verb) winken
we wir
weather das Wetter
wedding die Hochzeit
week die Woche
wellingtons die Gummistiefel
Welsh *(adj)* walisisch
  she's Welsh sie ist Waliserin
Welshman der Waliser
were: we were wir waren
  you were *(singular)*
    du warst *(familiar)*
    Sie waren *(polite)*
  you were *(plural)*
    ihr wart *(familiar)*
    Sie waren *(polite)*
west der Westen
West Germany die
  Bundesrepublik Deutschland
West Indian *(adj)* westindisch
West Indies Westindien
wet naß
what? was?
wheel das Rad
wheelchair der Rollstuhl
when? wann?
where? wo?
which? welche(r/s)?
whisky der Whisky

white weiß
who? wer?
why? warum?
wide weit
  (big) groß
wife die (Ehe)frau
wind der Wind
window das Fenster
windscreen die
  Windschutzscheibe
windscreen wiper der
  Scheibenwischer
wine der Wein
wine list die Weinkarte
wine merchant die
  Weinhandlung
wing der Flügel
with mit
without ohne
woman die Frau
wood *(forest)* der Wald
  (material) das Holz
wool die Wolle
word das Wort
work *(noun)* die Arbeit
  (verb) arbeiten
  (machine etc) funktionieren
worse schlechter

wrapping paper das Packpapier
  (for presents) das Geschenkpapier
wrist das Handgelenk
writing paper das Schreibpapier
wrong falsch

year das Jahr
yellow gelb
yes ja
yesterday gestern
yet: is it ready yet? ist es schon
  fertig?
  not yet noch nicht
yoghurt der Joghurt
you *(singular)* du *(familiar)*
  Sie *(polite)*
  (plural) Sie *(polite)*
your *(singular)* dein *(familiar)*
  Ihr *(polite)*
  (plural) euer *(familiar)*
  Ihr *(polite)*
youth hostel die Jugendherberge
zip der Reißverschluß
zoo der Zoo